LINFORD CHRISTIE

LINFORD

CHRISTIE

Duncan Mackay

Weidenfeld & Nicolson London

Contents

Record breaker: Christie beats Frankie Fredericks
(No. 2) and John Regis to set the first individual
world record of his career in Lievin, February 1995

fast

after all these years

Linford Christie, his muscles elbowed into submission by weeks of hard training in the warm Australian sunshine, settles into his starting blocks. He is wearing a lycra suit emblazoned with sponsors' logos which looks like it has been moulded on to him. The shoes are feather light, designed to give him that vital thousandth of a second advantage over his rivals. His hair is cropped close to his head and his eyes have the focused, haunted look of a man whose whole world depends on what happens during the next 20 seconds.

It is February 1995, and we are at the Meeting Vittel du Pas De Calais in Lievin for the finest, richest, most star-studded indoor event of the winter. There is already an electricity about the arena after the 7,000 capacity crowd have watched Russian Irina Privalova, Christie's female equivalent, narrowly miss breaking her own world record in the 60 metres and new American star Allen Johnson, the man who ended Colin Jackson's 44-race unbeaten streak, beat Britain's

Tony Jarrett in a photo-finish of the 60 metres hurdles.

Expectations are high that Namibia's Frankie Fredericks or Britain's John Regis, who are both running against Christie on this super-fast track, are capable of putting paid to the 200 metres world record of 20.36 set in this very stadium by Bruno-Marie Rose of France in 1987. Christie, six weeks short of his 35th birthday, is in the race only as an afterthought. His late request to be allowed to run had been granted by the French organizers only the previous evening. To accommodate him they have relegated the European champion Geir Moen of Norway to the B-race.

Christie's preparations have been far from ideal. He has not run a 200 metres for a year, and it had been midnight on Saturday before he had arrived from Vienna where he had competed the previous day and another 13 hours before his kit-bag with his spikes caught up with him after the airline lost his luggage. The 200 metres is also

Christie celebrates his record

Christie's least favourite event, which is ironic considering it was the one he had made his international breakthrough at in 1986. 'Too far to run' he has always insisted with a smile.

However, he has spent six weeks training with Fredericks in Australia and the distance's world indoor champion has suggested quite a number of refinements to Christie's technique which he believes might help him improve, especially around the bends where Christie has previously lost valuable hundredths of a second. He is keen to try them out before running before his own doting public in Birmingham the following Saturday.

A good omen for Christie had come 55 minutes earlier when he had set a European record of 6.47 seconds for 60 metres, a distance which favours those who like to get going in a hurry, not the likes of 6 foot 2 inch Christie who needs a few

> **The 200 metres is also Christie's least favourite event, which is ironic ... 'Too far to run' he has always insisted with a smile.**

strides to uncoil his long legs and get into his stride. 'He will break the world record in the 200 metres,' predicts Nelli Cooman, the great Dutch female indoor specialist, after she has watched the performance from the press benches.

Another excellent portent is that Christie has been given lane six, the outside one, for the race which is a single lap of the track. It is the same lane Rose set his record from in the European

(following page)
Splash it all over: Christie cools off

Indoor Championships, and where the angle of the turn is more gradual but the other runners are out of view until the home straight. Christie had watched from the stands the day Rose had established the record, nursing a hamstring injury.

He assumes his crouch for the race. Fredericks and Regis coil into theirs. Normally, Christie seems to roll out of his blocks the way one might roll of bed in the morning, but when the gun cracks today he gets an excellent start. Whether it is the spot on the outside which has made him wary of runners he cannot see, or his desire to compensate for a sore hamstring, he quickly opens up a gap over the two finest 200 metres runners in the world. He also runs the bends harder than usual. 'I didn't know what to expect,' he explained later. 'It was a case of going out and running.'

Regis is so astonished by what he is watching that he steps into Fredericks's lane and nearly gets tangled up with him. The graceful Namibian avoids him and desperately resumes the chase to catch Christie. But the realisation that he is a better teacher than a pupil dawns in the last few yards when he fails to catch Christie ('I could see his knees,' Christie admitted) who throws himself at the line.

All eyes dart to the electronic clock by the side of the track. It registers the figures '20.25' – a new world record by 0.11 of a second, a mile in sprinting terms. 'I used to think that you could always get Linford because he would fade after 150, but today he just surged on,' Fredericks said with a resigned shrug of the shoulders.

Christie has set the first individual world record of his career and become the first British sprinter to break a world record since 1960 when Peter Radford, the present chief executive of the British Athletic Federation, had set world records for 220 yards and 200 metres in the same race. Even in the extraordinary life and times of Linford Christie, it is a memorable moment, the fulfilment of a prophecy he had made eight years earlier when he said, 'I know that to be considered one of Britain's great athletes I must set a world record.' He was already, but now he's sharing a pedestal with the likes of Bannister, Coe, Ovett and Cram, world record breakers all.

By the time Christie had taken his two bouncy, jubilant, emotionally charged laps of honour

Tall guy: Christie is one of the world's tallest sprinters

Another medal, another medal ceremony: Linford Christie, Commonwealth 100 metres champion again, Victoria, August 1994

in Lievin, it was difficult to remember that just a few months earlier some people had spoken with conviction about how the years might be catching up with him. But Christie has demonstrated in a few seconds of brilliant running around the gentle curves of this famous oval in this tiny town in Flanders that those who claimed, 'He's only human – age must catch up with him one day. He can't keep on improving,' are wrong for another year at least.

Christie's record run pushed back the boundaries not only of athletic performance, but also of science. It was not only Christie's sprint rivals who were left shaking their heads at his performance. Many experts were forced to reassess their theories about the effects of ageing on performance. The conclusion they reached was that they may as well throw their research papers out of the window, Christie was rewriting the rule book.

He had not taken the sport seriously until he was 25, an age at which some former Olympic 100 metres champions were just quitting the sport, and now ten years later he was getting faster when everything these scientists had studied made them believe he should be sitting at home with his pipe and slippers.

After he finished second in the 1988 Olympics in Seoul, the magazine *Athletics Today* asked several experts whether they believed Christie could win the gold medal in Barcelona and, at the age of 32, become the oldest champion in history. The general consensus was that it was impossible. Sprinting is a young man's game.

Christie takes on American Dennis Mitchell, his biggest rival of 1994, in a controversial race at the IAAF Grand Prix Final, Paris

Not all researchers, however, were surprised by Christie's performance. 'If you stay highly motivated and injury-free and continue training at a decent intensity, you just don't lose very much,' explained Matthew Vukovich, a scientist at Ball State University in Indiana who had conducted a study on the subject. 'The main obstacle has simply been that runners believed they were too old to achieve such "miracles".'

According to Dr David Martin, an exercise physiologist from Georgia State University in Atlanta who monitored Sebastian Coe's training in the 1980s, Christie is getting better with age because of his ability to train correctly. 'If you use the Coe philosophy of less is more, it means you base your training around excellence rather than your injuries,' he said. 'Most research on ageing and performance had been done on sedentary people. But we know now that the more active you are, the later you can delay such deterioration.'

Christie is used to this fascination about his age, but unlike world heavyweight boxing champion George Foreman he is far from comfortable with the subject. More than one journalist has received a telephone call from him late at night or been on the wrong end of a tongue lashing at a press conference when he believes they have made too big an issue out of the subject. He once memorably told a press conference, 'Age is all in the mind. They say a male reaches his sexual peak at 19. How many of you guys believe that?' Put like that...

The latest estimate is that Christie will quit after defending his Olympic title in Atlanta next year, when he will be 36. But then in Seoul seven years ago he said he would probably retire after Barcelona in 1992. And following Barcelona he claimed he would hang up his spikes after running in the 1994 Commonwealth Games ('it doesn't matter how well or badly I'm running, that's it'). The truth is he is probably having so much fun and making so much money at the moment why should he even think about it? If the rest of the world is not comfortable about it, tough. That is his attitude.

But he admits, 'At a certain point it becomes like boxing. You see the young fighters coming up, sparring partners start to hurt you, pretty soon someone punches you flat out in the face and you think, 'Why am I doing this?' I'm not going out like that.'

With his performance in Lievin, Christie has laid down a pretty impressive marker for the summer. Athletics used to be a once every four years sport when the Olympic road show rolled into town. But now the circus is usually pitching the big top somewhere each year, and in 1995 it is at

The king meets the Prince: Linford discusses sprint technique and its finer points with HRH Prince Philip at Buckingham Palace

Old friends: Linford and Colin Jackson

the World Championships in Gothenburg, Sweden. The trash-talking Americans Carl Lewis, Leroy Burrell and Dennis Mitchell, who appropriately have helped turn sprinting into athletics' version of the world heavyweight boxing division, will hope to be there, ready to knock Christie off his perch.

What Lievin showed is that a world record breaking performance in the 100 metres is contained within Christie's body, awaiting release at the proper moment.

At the World Championships in Stuttgart two years ago, he ran 9.87 seconds – at the time just

Linford telling the world's press how it is at the World Championships, Stuttgart, August 1993

one hundredth of a second off the world record set by Lewis on a Tokyo track specifically designed to produce fast times. It stands now at 9.85 seconds to Lewis's Santa Monica Track Club colleague Burrell, but Christie is clearly physically capable of such a time.

No Briton has held the record outright for 73 years. The official Christie party line is that records are subservient to competitive performances. 'To be honest they don't bother me,' he said. 'Records are bound to be broken – championships stay forever.'

But after Lievin, Christie would dearly love to cap his career with the world 100 metres record, the most prestigious record in athletics. It would be the icing on a very big cake. Give him the right day, the right track, the right opposition, fill him full of the anger he uses as rocket fuel and watch him fly. Thirty-five years old. Who's counting?

CHAPTER 1

Finding
his feet

When he stood by his blocks for the opening heat of the 200 metres at the European Indoor Championships in Madrid in February 1986 thoughts of Olympic gold, world championship titles and world records were the furthermost thing from Linford Christie's mind. 'Just let me qualify for the next round,' he told himself.

Yank it up: a sign of things to come as Christie beats the Americans, RAF Cosford, 1986

Christie was not even considered the best British sprinter at these championships. It was Ade Mafe, at 19 six years Christie's junior but already with an Olympic final under his belt and the heir apparent to 1980 Olympic 100 metres champion Allan Wells, who was carrying that burden. But after he pulled a hamstring during the first round, Christie was suddenly Britain's only hope of a medal.

His early progress did not encourage optimism. He qualified from the first round only as a fastest loser and was second in his semi-final. Also, he was up against Aleksandr Yevgenyev, an indoor specialist who was a two-time winner of this title and the world indoor champion from the Soviet Union. The early stages of the race went to the script as Yevgenyev, in lane three, quickly swept passed Christie, in lane four, on the steeply banked 164 metre track.

But when the Soviet showed signs of flagging, Christie – who admitted afterwards he was expecting to settle for the silver or bronze medal – seized his opportunity. 'Yevgenyev was in my sights, coming off the last bend,' he explained to reporters afterwards. 'He seemed to relax and I just kicked.' A yard from the line, Christie threw his arms up in the air to celebrate his victory in 21.10 seconds and the world saw his winning smile for the first time. Linford Christie was the European Indoor 200 metres champion and, two months short of his 26th birthday, had arrived on the international scene.

The following week he appeared on the cover of *Athletics Weekly*, the sport's trade magazine, for the first time. 'It was an extraordinary performance by a man who had never before made any great mark in international running,' wrote Mel Watman. 'He has an excellent sprinting style and, with the added self-confidence the Madrid victory has given him, his attitude will be more positive.' Prophetic words.

'Certainly it surprised me,' he admitted in an interview with the magazine. 'Realistically, I only wanted to be better than the previous year in Athens, when I was dumped out in the first

Christie clinches the first major outdoor title of his career, the European Championships 100 metres, Stuttgart, 1986

turned out that the press had more faith in Christie's ability than Christie did himself at this stage of his career.

Victory at the European Indoor Championships had made Christie sit down and think about what he could achieve. 'At first he hadn't taken sprinting that seriously, but when he beat that Soviet runner, it all changed,' recalled his father, James. 'He told me it was something different. It was his first major gold medal and it made him believe in himself.'

It was coach Ron Roddan

'... that's the advantage of being the underdog ... the worst you can do is come up to expectations'

round. I had nothing to lose, that's the advantage of being the underdog ... the worst you can do is come up to expectations ... or down to them.'

In view of Christie's later relationship with the press – who he is continually complaining do not support him enough – it is worth noting that after his victory in Madrid several newspapers were predicting great things for him. 'I'd love to believe what the papers say about my capabilities this summer,' he said, 'but I'd be fool if I did.' It

who, in a letter which has since become legendary throughout the athletics world, had provided Christie with a kick up the backside when his casual approach threatened to leave his talent unfulfilled. While other less talented athletes were slogging their guts out training at West London Stadium, Christie would often prefer to retreat to Mick's Café, adjacent to the track, and play dominoes with his friends.

James Christie also put pressure on his son to

per week, plus £2,000 arrears.

'Linford wanted to do it but didn't want to train for it,' explained Roddan. 'He just wouldn't come training and only did it when he felt like it. He would party at weekends and sometimes a group of them would come straight to training on a Sunday morning from a party which had just finished.'

Les Hoyte, the star of Roddan's training group at the time and the man who gave Christie his first pair of running spikes, can remember having to knock on Christie's door to get him to come out and train. 'We had to keep at him because we didn't want to see his natural talent wasted,' he revealed to the *News of the World*. 'Linford felt guilty when he saw us. So he would rouse himself and get down to some hard work.

'Also, Linford hated the idea of doing weights in the early days. He was always a pretty smart dresser and was bothered about growing too big to get into his shirts. I had to egg him on, challenge him to beat me at weights.

'But I always knew he was talented. I told anyone who would listen that Linford Christie would be the man one day. People would ask me to put my money where my mouth was at various meetings. And I admit I did lose a few quid before Linford made his breakthrough.'

'I would stay out pretty late some nights,' Christie admits, 'and I used to take two or three weeks off running just because I thought I needed a rest. Then Ron wrote to me saying if I didn't come back now, I was not to come back at all! I came back.'

Around the same time, Christie also received a letter from Andy Norman. Norman, a police sergeant at Penge, was the most powerful man in British athletics and the paymaster. He had guided Steve Ovett's career and could make or break an athlete's career. If you upset Norman, then you were out. But if you had talent coupled with enthusiasm and dedication, then the sky was the limit as far as he was concerned.

'Andy told me I could become the best sprinter in Europe if I changed my life style. What with that and friends threatening not to take me to parties any more, I changed my attitude.'

But if Norman ever felt Christie was slipping back into his old ways, he was not adverse to administering another swift reminder to him to

buckle down. 'If you want something, go ahead and do it,' he told him. 'All you think about is women. Think about sprinting and the gold medal is yours. Don't get old saying you should have done it.'

When he was 19, Christie had become a father for the first time. Six years later, just as he was making an impact at international level, he got a different woman pregnant. The couple split up before she gave birth to twins.

Christie refused to pay maintenance for the twins until 1990 when DNA genetic tests proved he was the father and he was ordered to pay £60

ensure he kept his nose to the grindstone. On one famous occasion he gave Christie's lane away hours before a big race at Crystal Palace, ringing him up and telling him, 'Don't bother turning up – you're not running.'

On another occasion when a young Christie was travelling home from a second division meeting in Finland he complained to Norman about his flight arrangements. In athletics the style you travel in is determined by your world ranking, and as Christie was ranked in the hundreds he was expected to travel whichever way he was told. 'Don't you fucking tell me how you want to travel,' said Norman. 'You couldn't fill a telephone box.' The bullying he received at the hands of Norman only made him more determined to succeed, which was the idea.

Old schoolboy rivals remember Christie boasting as a teenager that he could be 'Britain's best ever sprinter'. 'Everyone said I was talking rubbish,' admitted Christie. 'After I came second in the English Schools in 1979 – behind Phil Brown – I came up against guys who were already established internationals and knew something about training. I didn't and I used to get my kicks

out of beating them when I was basically foolin' around.'

But natural talent will only get you so far and Christie's career soon stuttered to a halt amid complaints that he was being overlooked by the selectors unfairly. In 1984, he was controversially overlooked for a place in Britain's team for the Los Angeles – even for the 4x100 metres sprint relay team – and was shattered. In 1985 he was so upset at being left out of Britain's European Cup team he angrily confronted the secretary of the British Amateur Athletic Board Nigel Cooper and chief coach Frank Dick in their London office.

It ended with Christie pushing Dick and telling him, 'The only reason I won't punch you is that I don't want to come down to your level.'

And Christie's mood was certainly not helped when, as he was leaving, Cooper said, 'It's good to be angry, Linford. It shows you care.'

'There were times when I felt like packing the whole thing in,' he admitted after he had finally achieved his breakthrough. 'There were times when I expected to be selected and I wasn't. When I didn't get to the European Cup in Moscow, it nearly killed me off. I was close to breaking point. I nearly said, "Stuff it".

'I felt I was so naturally talented that nothing else was needed. Then I was made to understand that there were other guys with plenty of natural talent who were prepared to do enough extra work to edge me out. That was when it became a job for me.'

Today, Christie says he has no regrets about his 'wasted' years. 'A lot of the 18-year-olds and 20-year-olds who are coming along now, and living for nothing but athletics, cannot hope to last as long as I have. When they get to 25 they will realize they have missed out on their youth and it will be hard to maintain the 100 per cent dedication that athletics at the top demands. I enjoyed

British chief coach Frank Dick was not such a popular figure with Christie

The old and the new: Christie beats Scotland's 1980 Olympic 100 metres champion Allan Wells, IAC Miller Lite meeting, Edinburgh, 1987

my youth to the full and now I don't have any hunger for the things that could tempt those youngsters away.'

Christie had nearly always shown promise, though it was not immediately apparent from his debut on the track. His first race in his primary school sports day was at the famous White City Stadium, the spiritual home of British athletics. He wore 'Alf Ramsey shorts and black plimsolls' but trailed in towards the back in the 100 yards race.

But as he ran more regularly in secondary school, his talent began to manifest itself. PE teacher Derek Jones, at Henry Compton Comprehensive School in Hammersmith, encouraged him because he saw athletic potential in this gawky teenager who was talented but on the lazy side. 'He got me to run when I'd much rather have been doing something else,' said Christie.

'He made me keen.'

Linford Ecerio Christie was born in St Andrews, Jamaica, on 2 April 1960, the middle child among four sisters and two brothers. His parents emigrated to England in 1962 and his father worked at a factory making baths, saving enough from his £3-a-week wages so he could eventually bring the rest of the family over from Jamaica. Christie's grandmother, Anita Morrison, brought him up in Kingston until he was seven when he joined his mother and father in a house in Loftus Road, just a free kick away from Queens Park Rangers Football Club.

When he arrived in England it was the middle of winter. 'I remember seeing snow for the first time and running out to play in it,' recalled Christie. 'It soon started burning my fingers and toes. I'd never experienced such cold in my life. It was a shock to my system.'

Another shock was rejoining the mother he had forgotten, Mabel. 'Dad introduced me to a woman, saying, "This is your mum". I thought, "No, granny is my mum". I don't think I loved anybody as much as I loved her. When I won the European 200 metres I dedicated it to her.'

Christie left school at 16 to attend an electronics course at Wandsworth Technical College, but he soon decided to get a job so he could get some money. He got a job as an accounts clerk with the Co-op, studying at evening classes for five O-levels so he could pursue a dream of joining the civil service. 'I love the smell of money,' he admits. 'But I hated it at the Co-op. You had to work Saturdays and it got in the way of my athletics. I became a youth worker as it enabled me to train when I wanted.

'Then I went into local government, working for the community relations advisor at Kensington Town Hall. After that I was a sports co-ordinator but in the end none of it was for me. So I left to do athletics full-time.'

Having taken the plunge to commit himself to an athletics career, Christie was on the verge of the fast track to athletics immortality, having changed from being an 'avid party-goer, often coming home with the milkman, and a devotee of rum and blackcurrant and Babycham' into a determined, devoted perfectionist of the track.

And there was no man better qualified to guide Christie's

career than Ron Roddan. The former club standard quarter miler had devoted half his life to coaching athletes after stumbling into the profession by accident when his own trainer, Arthur Filkins, at Thames Valley Harriers had to retire through ill health. 'I was the oldest in the group; they looked at me and said, "You'll carry on, won't you".' From Michael Hauck, a 47.4 400

metres runner, on to Dick Steane, who set a British 200 metres record of 20.66 seconds in 1968, and then through to international sprinters Les and Wendy Hoyte, he had always worked with top class athletes.

Roddan, a 63-year-old bachelor who took early retirement from the Geological Society four years ago, can still remember meeting Christie for the first time in 1979. 'He had a big bushy Afro hairstyle,' he says. 'So did Daley Thompson. It was the fashion.'

Each day, as the bitter winds blew across the wide expanse of Wormwood Scrubs and down the home straight of West London Stadium, Roddan would coach Christie. Curious passers-by would watch the strange sight of Christie sprinting with a waist-harness and dragging along a heavy tyre attached to it. It was all part of Christie's plan to get stronger so that he could translate his winter form into summer fulfilment.

As Christie himself admitted, the European indoor title was a nice thing to win, but he had to prove himself over the 'real thing' outdoors, especially the 100 metres. He did that in June when he returned to Madrid for a meeting and ran 10.04 seconds, taking seven-hundredths of a second off the UK record Allan Wells had set at the Moscow Olympics in 1980. It was an astonishing jump up in class for someone who had only improved from 10.7 to 10.42 between 1979 and 1985.

In July, at the ill-fated Edinburgh Commonwealth Games – which had been badly hit by an African boycott over Britain's links with South Africa – Christie became the first Englishman to take a medal in the 100 metres since Cyril Holmes won the title in 1938. But he was no match for another Jamaican immigrant, a Canadian called Ben Johnson, who streaked to

'Are you looking at us?' – Linford Christie and 1984 Olympic javelin champion Tessa Sanderson

victory in 10.07 seconds to Christie's 10.28.

Christie was now clearly established as Europe's number one sprinter, but Allan Wells was hanging on for dear life to his career. At 34 the Scotsman had confounded the critics when he beat Johnson at a post-Commonwealth Games meeting in Gateshead and qualified for the European Championships in Stuttgart.

He was no match for Christie in the Neckar Stadium, however. Christie was untouchable, setting a championship record of 10.15 seconds as Wells finished fifth. He had expected nothing less, displaying far more confidence in his ability than he had just six months earlier in Madrid. 'I would have thrown away a silver or bronze medal,' he said. 'I wanted only gold.'

Afterwards, Christie paid a long and fulsome tribute to Wells' contribution to the sport in Britain. 'He's the godfather of British sprinting,' he said. 'He has shown us we can take on the Americans and beat them.'

For a born again athlete in the embryonic days of his international career, Wells was a particular inspiration and someone to model yourself on. A former long jumper, he had not turned seriously to sprinting until he was 24. 'He knows about producing the goods on the day,' he told *Athletics Weekly*. 'He's been doing it consistently for years. You've got to admire a guy who can peak as successfully as he has over the years. He trains bloody hard too – much more than myself.'

Madrid and Stuttgart may have seen Christie take the first steps towards sprinting on to millionaires row but that was still a long way away. At this time, life remained a financial struggle. In his first season, when Christie was unable to meet his £50-a-week physiotherapist bills out of his dole cheque, he survived on handouts from his girlfriend, Mandy Miller, and was grateful for the meals her mother used to feed him.

Centre of attention: Linford Christie takes on Ernest Obeng (right) and world record holder Calvin Smith, Nice, 1987

'In the end I was so desperate I rang Capital Radio to see if they could help me,' said Christie. 'The guy laughed. He really couldn't believe I had no money. But they invited me to be interviewed and I said what I wanted most was the use of a car. A listener phoned and said he had a poster company and would I like a Nissan? He was my first sponsor.'

His new status as European champion did not impress the gateman at his training track (which would one day be renamed the 'Linford Christie Stadium') either. When he asked whether he would be able to use the track free now, they told him he would still have to pay his 40 pence per day entrance fee. 'Tight sods,' he labelled them.

As well as giving him handouts and feeding him, Mandy Miller, the woman with whom Christie was soon to settle down, also persuaded a cosmetics company to sponsor him on a warm weather training trip to Lanzarote.

'I'm still grateful to her for that,' he said. 'That really helped me. All the money in the world wouldn't compensate for what I've put in.

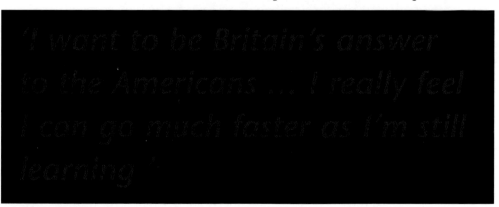

'I want to be Britain's answer to the Americans ... I really feel I can go much faster as I'm still learning.'

I've slogged and sweated for every penny. '

At the end of 1986, Christie had risen from 200th in the world rankings to fourth behind Americans Carl Lewis, Calvin Smith and Ben Johnson. By now, his confidence had grown to match his talent. 'I want to be Britain's answer to the Americans,' he said. 'I really feel I can go

to 1981 when Christie was only 20 and Dick accused him of going behind his back to gain selection for an international. 'I felt really small,' Christie later told *Athletics Today*. 'I didn't realize people could talk to each other like that. We never really got on after that. Another time in Birmingham a few of us were talking when he came up to me and said, "You'll never make it. Why don't you take up long jumping or something?"'

The friction had escalated over the years with Christie blaming Dick for his non-selection for Los Angeles and the 1985 European Cup. Rome was the first of several major arguments the pair were to have regarding the relay over the next few years. But this was the biggest event Christie had ever run in and the ill-feeling could not have helped his concentration.

'There was a lot said in the British press about the row,' he told *Athletics Canada*. 'Their side, my side and the truth. The clash of personalities with Dick and the bad press was something I could have done without in my build up to the final.'

In the event, Christie acquitted himself magnificently in the 'sprint race of the century'. Carl Lewis and Ben Johnson had been racing each other since 1980 when their paths had crossed for the first time in a junior international. For five years Lewis had comfortably held the upper hand, winning the 1983 World Championships and 1984 Olympics, but in 1985 Johnson beat Lewis in Zurich, thereby laying the seeds for a rivalry which grew more intense and bitter with each meeting.

In Rome, Johnson simply destroyed Lewis with an awesome display which will linger long in the memory of anyone who saw it. His time of 9.83 seconds took a full tenth of a second off Calvin Smith's world record – a furlong in sprinting terms. Lewis equalled the old record of 9.93 while Jamaica's Ray Stewart finished third in 10.08 with Christie fourth in 10.14, pulling up as he approached the finish line with an attack of cramp. 'It was a privilege to be part of such a momentous race,' Christie told reporters afterwards. He was not disappointed.

A few days later, Lewis let his frustrations pour out. In an interview with ITV, he claimed that he knew of several athletes at these World Championships using performance-enhancing

much faster as I'm still learning.'

His meteoric progress continued the following year and after completing a European Cup 100 and 200 metres double in Prague and lowering the British 100 metres record to 10.03 seconds in Budapest he should have travelled to Rome for the World Championships on a psychological high. However, a public blazing row with Frank Dick at the training track in Rome over the composition of the 4x100 metres relay squad badly disrupted his preparations.

It was the culmination of a long-running feud between Christie and Dick which dated back

Rome was an ill-tempered championship all round for Christie, because it was here that his dislike of the press – which has gradually grown with each passing year of his career – really began to express itself. 'They wrote I was cracking up because I saw Ben and Carl in the village,' he complained in *Athletics Weekly* in 1987. 'There were people in Rome who did a lot worse than me and they weren't put down half as much. All I get is a headache and I don't need it.

'If they were gossip columnists then fair enough, but they call themselves sports writers. It's wrong and I can't come to terms with it. The press never take the time to get to know me and the thing that annoys me the most is before I used to always find time to talk to them. No-one can win in this situation but unless they start being more favourable towards me it's going to stay like that.'

This year was also significant for something which seemed relatively minor at the time, but would become an important part of the Christie legend in the years to come. In 1986, Allan Wells had taken to wearing cycling shorts because he believed they offered his fragile hamstrings more protection against the cold than the traditional running pants.

> ## 'If they were gossip columnists then fair enough, but they call themselves sports writers'

At the European Indoor Championships in 1987 in Lievin, Christie had pulled his hamstring. When he returned for the summer he too adopted the 'longs', which were made of lycra. The new style shorts quickly became all the rage among the sprinting fraternity, drawing new female fans to the 100 and 200 metres. But in one interview, Christie complained, 'Some guys have made it disgusting, though, with nothing on underneath. I like some kind of decency.'

substances. No names were mentioned, but the implication was obvious: Carl Lewis had lost the World Championship because Ben Johnson had been taking drugs. Lewis was dismissed as a poor loser.

Seoul
searching

Shining light: Linford obliges autograph hunters, RAF Cosford, 1988

It was the race that never officially happened, but will go down in history as the most famous in Olympic history. And it was the Olympic Games which nearly ruined Linford Christie's career. Yes, the 1988 Seoul Olympics certainly turned out to be a memorable experience for everybody.

The only place to start is at the beginning. Christie had put the trauma of Rome behind him and prepared meticulously all summer. For his final build-up, he had paid for coach Ron Roddan to fly to the Nihon training camp out of his own pocket so he could add the finishing touches to his preparations. The British team were sharing the camp with the Americans, including Carl Lewis, Edwin Moses and Florence Griffith-Joyner, in the Japanese countryside, 60 miles from Tokyo, well away from the security threat of South Korea.

Meanwhile, fuelled by Carl Lewis's accusations in Rome that Ben Johnson was on drugs, relations between the world's two fastest men had

become even more hostile. 'They're about as friendly as Iran and Iraq,' remarked *Time* magazine.

Christie had been singing Johnson's praises in the run-up to the Olympics, but complaining about the lack of respect he had received from Lewis. 'I don't respect him 'cause he's got no manners,' Christie told *Athletics Weekly*. 'I think if you don't respect the guy who comes last in the race, you shouldn't be there. Carl did an interview in Rome last year and he said, "Who's this guy Linford Christie, does he think he's got a chance?"

'That's why I want to beat him. The Americans don't believe a European will ever dominate the sprints and the worst thing is everyone believes them. But Americans can be beaten and that's something I really want to prove over the next few years.'

'The Americans don't believe a European will ever dominate the sprints ... and everyone believes them'

Unlike in Rome, Christie had managed to avoid getting involved in big conflicts with Frank Dick and was concentrating all his energies on the race on this occasion. He looked comfortable in the heats, emerging as a potential medallist in the semi-final when he ran 10.11 seconds to finish second to Johnson's 10.03. It was Lewis who had caught the eye in the opening three rounds, however, progressing through the preliminaries with times of 9.99, 10.17 and 9.97 seconds.

Johnson had not been in the form of 1987. He had an acrimonious split from his mentor and coach Charlie Francis, only to patch up the relationship a few days later. He had struggled to deal with a hamstring injury which had dogged him all year and been beaten easily by Lewis at a big pre-Olympic big money showdown in Zurich. 'It's not been a good time,' he had admitted when he arrived in Seoul.

But in the final before a television audience of half-a-billion he turned on his full awesome power. When the gun fired for the start he leapt out of his blocks and was quickly into his running. As he burst across the line, he thrust the extended index finger of his right hand high into the air. His time was an unbelievable 9.79 seconds, taking another four hundredths of a second off his own world record – a mark which he had claimed only a year earlier would stand as long as Bob Beamon's long jump world record. Three times in the last 30 metres of the race Lewis looked across at Johnson, hardly believing what he was seeing, his face growing more confused and angry with each stolen glance.

After the race was over, Lewis ran over to Johnson, pawing at his shoulder and finally twisting him round to bestow a handshake on the man who had succeeded him as Olympic champion. It was all good PR for the American but what Lewis was actually thinking at the time, he later admitted in his autobiography, was, 'The bastard has done it to me again.'

Lewis, himself, had run faster than in Rome – but lost by more. He clocked 9.92 to break his own American record. And then came Christie. Running superbly, he finished third in 9.97 seconds. It made him the first European ever to break 10 seconds for the 100 metres and installed him as the sixth fastest man in history. He was not surprisingly ecstatic.

'A lot of people had doubted me,' he wrote in his autobiography, published in 1989. 'Now here I was in the greatest race of all time, with four men under ten seconds. I wanted to show all these people who had mocked and doubted. Standing around at the finish, I remembered them all.'

Sixty-nine hours later the shocking news was announced which was to cast a shadow over the achievement. Michele Verdier of the International Olympic Committee faced a packed auditorium with lights, television cameras, microphones, reporters jostling for a position. In a sombre tone she announced, 'The urine sample of Ben Johnson, Canada, athletics, 100 metres, collected on Saturday, 24th September 1988, was found to contain the metabolites of a banned substance, namely stanozolol, an anabolic steroid.' The fastest man in the world was a junkie.

With Ben Johnson disqualified, Lewis was now promoted to first place and Christie suddenly found himself the silver medallist. Three days earlier, believing he had finished third, Christie had been bubbling over with enthusiasm. 'I have trained all year for this ... It was my dream to run under 10 seconds ... I knew I had broken the European record ... It's the greatest moment of my life.' The words had rolled from his mouth almost as fast as he had run.

But when he was woken up in the athletes village by British officials Tony Ward and Les Jones to be told the news he was stunned. Johnson was a friend. How could he have done this? Why? Surely there had been some mistake? There were plenty of questions, but no answers. BBC TV and ITV asked him to do interviews, but he looked uncomfortable sitting in a studio on his own, in a chair with his head bowed, staring

Linford enjoys a joke, McVities Challenge, 1988

at a monitor on the floor as he answered questions from London. What could he say?

In his autobiography, Christie described how his own emotions tumbled out when he met one of the Canadian sprint coaches later in the day. 'I cried for Ben because I felt so sorry for him,' he wrote. 'I have always argued that anyone who is found positive should be banned for life, but you always hope it's not going to happen to someone you know. I cried because it hurt. It was a sad, sad day.

'I wasn't crying only for Ben Johnson, I was crying for my sport. I love my athletics. It is the vehicle that has enabled me to express myself, it is the only thing that I have ever been really good at – I was never going to be a world class scholar or musician or anything. Sprinting has given me self respect, taken me out of the ruck. It is my business. And now, I thought, it is the end of athletics as we know it.'

In his *Athletics Today* column in January 1989, Christie wrote, 'I had no idea he was on drugs. Of course, I'd heard rumours, but if you listened to rumours you'd never get out of bed in the morning. The trouble is just as it used to be if you owned a black cat you were a witch, now if you run you are supposed to be on drugs. It has got out of hand.'

He elaborated further in another interview in 1989, saying, 'I still feel sorry for Ben. I don't think any drug you can take can actually make you run as fast as he did. Ben was always good to me and I've learned a lot from him – about starting technique and things like that. He was a big star and he didn't have to talk to people like me.'

Christie, however, has been a consistent campaigner on the dangers of taking performance enhancing substances and, to reinforce the point he is clean, regularly wears T-shirts with slogans like 'No Additives' and 'Pure Talent' printed on them. As drugs controversies continued to dog the sport in Britain through 1994 thanks to the Diane Modahl and Paul Edwards doping scandals, in an interview with Sky Sports he toughened his stance even further when he said not only did he believe all steroid users should be banned for life but they should be sent to prison.

'If people want to take the risk they should face the consequences,' he said. 'They can hang them for all I care. The sentence doesn't affect me

High fashion: Linford and John Regis, Dairy Crest Games, 1988

sort of accusation hits and hurts. I'm glad that I'm drug free, and I swear that on my grandmother's grave. And she was the dearest person to me.'

Christie has often told interviewers who have asked him about drugs, 'When I die they can perform an autopsy on me and they will find that I have never ever taken an illegal substance. I know that if I suddenly start feeling pains anywhere in my body, I don't have to worry that it is the side effects of drugs, as, regrettably, some athletes do.'

Therefore, as Christie sat in the television studio in Seoul, he could never have imagined that before he had the opportunity to collect the silver medal he had originally been cheated out of, he too would soon have the noose around his neck. He thought nothing of it when he was selected for a random drugs test following the final of the 200 metres, after all he was always being asked to pee into a bottle. It was part and parcel of being a world class athlete and, unlike Johnson, he knew he had nothing to fear. He had given a clean sample after the 100 metres final.

But when his sample was tested something illegal showed up. It contained 8.4 parts to the 1 million of pseudo-ephedrine, a stimulant which carried a three month suspension. The actual amount found was a minute figure, hardly enough to register a reading and certainly not enough to assist anyone's performance. However, as soon as the hare is out the trap and running, news of a positive drugs test can spread quicker than a bush fire in an Olympic city – and rumours were soon circulating about Christie. It appeared to be another major Olympic drugs scandal.

(facing page)
We have lift off

because I don't take drugs. People who take drugs believe what they are doing is right, they believe everybody is doing it.'

In 1987 *The Times* ran a series of articles alleging drug abuse was rife in British athletics. Christie had, understandably, taken an exception to one of the articles in which it was claimed that one sprinter had said that if you were not on drugs it was like racing in plimsolls against everyone else in spikes. The implication was pretty clear.

'I think whoever said that is wrong,' he told the writer, Pat Butcher. 'I've got where I am through hard work, and hard work alone. That

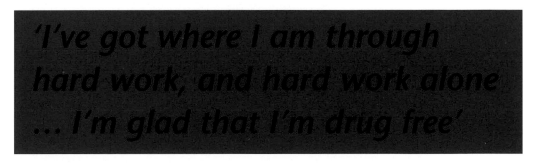

'I've got where I am through hard work, and hard work alone ... I'm glad that I'm drug free'

He was asked to attend the testing of the B-sample of his drug, as was another British competitor, judo player Kerrith Brown whose test after his bronze medal was also under scrutiny. The result was the same. Christie was then

and back. I was so close to suicide, I really was.'

The incident left Christie with deep scars, as he explained in an interview with *Woman* magazine. 'The doctors said that the minute amount of ephedrine in my system couldn't have enhanced my performance,' he said. 'But they never actually said in so many words at the time so I think it left a few people thinking, "Well, there's no smoke without fire".

'But ginseng is a natural health product. The Chinese swear by it. I didn't take it to make me run faster but simply for my general well being. You've got to be so careful. Three cups of black coffee or too much Coca Cola can put so much

quizzed for 18 hours by officials who demanded to know what he had taken. He told the committee that it must have come from drinking large amounts of ginseng, a Korean elixir, which contained pseudo-ephedrine. He had drunk it after his 100 metres race and before the 200 metres. Christie had asked the British team doctors about taking ginseng and they had not told him there was anything potentially wrong with the substance.

In fact, the reading on the sample was so low that it should not have even constituted a positive test and Christie was eventually given the 'benefit of the doubt' – an unfortunate choice of words by Prince Alexandre de Merode, the Belgian chairman of the IOC's Medical Commission, which angered the International Amateur Athletic Federation who insisted that Christie had done nothing wrong and was totally in the clear. By this time, though, the results of his tests had already been published around the world and his name tarnished.

'When they said my test was positive I was very, very worried,' Christie said. 'I even felt guilty. And yet I knew I wasn't. I had to keep telling myself, "You're innocent". I went to hell

caffeine in your system that you run the risk of being banned. But I think 99.9 per cent of the British people know I'm clean. They know I've been one of the most outspoken people against drugs in athletics.'

This storm in a ginseng tea cup which brewed around Christie totally detracted from the fact he had finished fourth in the final of the 200 metres,

(facing page)
Focused

Linford with his Olympic bronze medal. No-one realized the biggest scandal in Olympic history was just hours away

them.' Under oath at a Canadian government inquiry headed by Ontario's associate chief justice Charles Dubin, Johnson finally admitted that he had used steroids and that he had been knowingly taking them since 1984.

Johnson's confession forced the IAAF to retrospectively alter their record books. So his 'world record' of 9.83 he had set in Rome was scrubbed and he was disqualified from the race, meaning Christie was promoted to the bronze medal position. The Commonwealth Games Federation also were to later disqualify Johnson from the 1986 event in Edinburgh and to award the title to Christie.

When he returned from Seoul, Christie sat down with Ron Roddan and planned where they should go from here. While many people saw it as being the pinnacle of Christie's career, Roddan saw it as only the beginning. 'He can get faster,

The model sprinter

an outstanding performance from a man who had never been fully at ease with the distance. He finished only half-a-metre behind the bronze medallist Robson da Silva of Brazil and his personal best of 20.09 was nine hundredths of a second inside John Regis's UK record and ranked him third on the European all-time list.

A bitter-sweet Olympic Games ended on a high note for Christie when, 24 hours after being cleared, his blistering last leg in the 4x100 metres relay lifted Britain's team from fifth place to the silver medals, only failing to catch the Soviet Union quartet by a metre. 'I ran that leg,' he said afterwards, 'on sheer frustration.' But the sense of irony was not lost on him when he was 'selected' to represent Britain's team and take a drugs test afterwards.

Johnson had returned to Canada in shame, but he continued to deny that he had ever knowingly taken drugs. Angela Issajenko, Canada's leading female sprinter and a former training partner of Johnson's in the Charlie Francis stable, was angry by his denials. She told the newspapers, 'Ben takes steroids. I take steroids. Nobody takes steroids without knowing they are taking

(facing page) Linford receives the baton from Marcus Adam, European Cup, Gateshead, 1989

CHAPTER 3

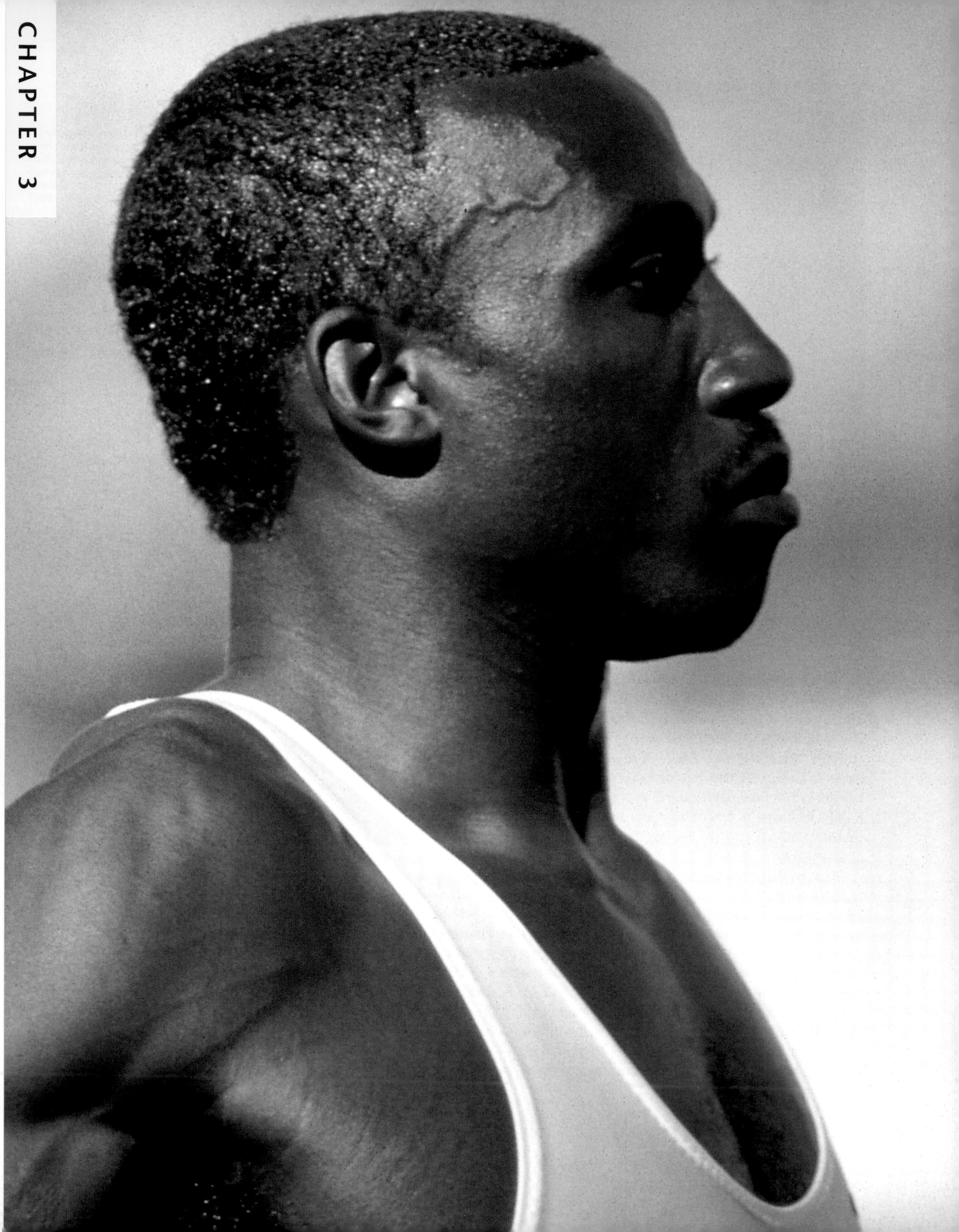

So near
... yet so far

The Santa Monica Track Club is probably the most famous organisation of its kind in athletics today. The club was founded by Joe Douglas and has a group of world class sprinters who would walk into most national teams. In 1991, it had on its books, in addition to Carl Lewis, Mark Witherspoon, a former American 100 metres champion, Floyd Heard, a former world number one at 200 metres, Joe DeLoach, the 1988 Olympic 200 metres champion, Steve Lewis, the Olympic 400 metres champion, and Leroy Burrell, the new up and coming young sprinter on the world scene.

After Lewis made such a huge impact at the World Championships in Helsinki in 1983 by winning gold medals in the 100 metres, long jump and 4x100 metres relay he immediately became the hottest property in athletics, the man every meeting had to have. That meant Douglas could ask up to $30,000 per meeting for Lewis to appear, including all the trappings like first class travel and accommodation in a five star hotel. But on the back of Lewis, meetings had to take other Santa Monica runners who they may not have wanted. The deal was simple: take Lewis and Santa Monica, or take nothing at all.

Down the years, this policy has attracted the club many critics, especially from race promoters and rivals who resent the fact that they believe Santa Monica's athletes are receiving preferential treatment. 'Promoters tell me they can't have a meeting without Carl or Leroy,' said Joe Douglas. 'What should I do? Let them have them free. I don't think we should be blamed for being more marketable. That's the nature of the world.'

Douglas once boasted that Lewis 'makes more money than the rest of the track and field world combined', and he may have been only half joking. While persistent rumours circulating that he was gay may have hurt his marketability after his four gold medals in the 1984 Los Angeles Olympics (equalling the number the legendary Jesse Owens had won in Berlin in 1936), he had a shoe contract with Mizuno worth $1.7 million and had world-wide deals to endorse various products, including cars, a non-athletic shoe company and watches. After Seoul, he had even released a pop record which reached number one in the Swedish charts, though it flopped almost everywhere else.

Black and proud – Commonwealth Games, Auckland, 1990

Christie wins the 60 metres from Pierfrancesco Pavoni of Italy at the 1990 European Indoor Championships, Glasgow

Burrell had long been viewed as Lewis's successor even before he broke his team-mate's world 100 metres record of 9.92 seconds at the 1991 USA/Mobil Championships at New York in June. Enjoying the run of his career, Burrell clocked 9.90 with the aid of a 1.9 metres per second wind (the legal limit is 2 metres per second, after that records are wind assisted) to beat Lewis by three-hundredths of a second. Many people regarded the moment as the crown passed from the head of Lewis, who turned 30 on 1 July, to the young pretender, Burrell, who was still only 24.

What few people knew was that Lewis had missed valuable training time before New York because he had been working as a sports director on KHYS, a Houston radio station, and writing his autobiography, *Inside Track*. However, his time was still the second fastest of his career, showed that he was still a major contender and it was too

early to write him off yet, especially with the World Championships coming up in Tokyo. Unlike Lewis, who had always seemed destined for athletic success from an early age, Burrell had come to sprinting in unusual fashion. A baseball coach at Penwood High School, Philadelphia, had told him, 'Leroy, you can't hit anything and you can't catch anything. But you sure can run bases. Go off and work out for the track team.'

In every other sense, Burrell seemed to be a clone of Carl Lewis. Burrell came from Pennsylvania, the same as Lewis; Burrell competed for the University of Houston, where Lewis studied; Burrell ran for Santa Monica Track Club, like Lewis; Burrell was managed by Joe Douglas, who was Lewis's manager; Burrell was coached by Tom Tellez, Lewis's long-time coach; Burrell studied Communications and Radio TV at university, which had been Lewis's subject.

Perhaps that is why Linford Christie dislikes him so much. In February 1991, in the final international meeting to be staged in RAF Cosford's old hangar, the two had an altercation at the end of the 60 metres. Burrell, who four days earlier had set a new world indoor record for the distance of 6.46 seconds, accused Christie of making a post-race threat. Christie was angry because half-way through the race Burrell had turned towards him and eye-balled him.

As they walked off the track, they exchanged angry words. 'He threatened to kill me,' said Burrell. 'He said, "If you do that again, I will hurt you, I will kill you." So I said to him, "Then kill me now".' The two had to be separated by meeting promoter Andy Norman, who led Christie away. It was a sad and undignified way for Christie to say farewell to an arena which had given him so many happy memories.

'Before I was in track, I was never aggressive,' explained Christie when asked about the incident later. 'It's like going to war. Soldiers aren't necessarily born killers. It's their trade. You are taught to kill your enemy. Away from athletics I'm a totally different person. I don't take my work home. I leave it on the track.'

Frank Dick, Britain's former chief coach who has probably had more rows with Christie than anyone, was able to explain why the incident happened, what makes the fast men tick. 'The nearest thing to a world class sprinter is a thoroughbred racehorse,' he said. 'They have the same prickliness. They're highly tuned, on the edge all the time.'

Both sprinters later apologised to each other – Burrell: 'I shouldn't have done it.' Christie: 'I over-reacted' – but it betrayed how deeply Christie disliked not only Burrell but American sprinters in general (especially ones who were more successful than him). In 1990, he had won

Stretching out

the 10,000 metres all the more praiseworthy. The Scot ran away from the finest women's field assembled to win the biggest title of her career just nine months after coming back from pregnancy. But McColgan's victory was nothing compared to the 100 metres, a race *Runner's World* magazine called the 'finest footrace ever run over any distance'. They were not kidding either.

It was just after seven o'clock in the evening as the eight finest sprinters in the world settled into their blocks for the final. The stadium was full with 60,000 spectators, including the Emperor and Empress of Japan, some of the world's top sumo wrestlers and Ben Johnson.

In 1989, Johnson had dropped his claims of innocence and admitted taking steroids to the Dubin Inquiry. Then, having completed his suspension in October 1990, he had made a well-publicized and lucrative comeback during the indoor season of 1991. He had then picked up a cheque for $75,000 for racing Lewis in a 'grudge'

the Commonwealth and European 100 metres titles in Auckland and Split respectively, but his superiority had not been seriously challenged in these areas since 1986 and it was a bit like Manchester United winning the GM Vauxhall Conference League.

But in 1991, Christie had been trying for several years to ascend to the summit, to become world number one, coming close when he won his Olympic silver medal. However, when he saw Burrell emerge from the Lewis stable he must have been close to accepting that perhaps he was destined never to achieve that target.

Indeed, when Christie arrived in Tokyo for the World Championships he must have wondered if he was ever destined to win a major title on the global stage. Earlier in the year, he had gone to Seville for the World Indoor Championships but even in the absence of Burrell could not win. He finished second in the 60 and 200 metres, losing to another American, Andre Cason, and a Bulgarian, Nikolay Antonov, who he had always beaten comfortably outdoors.

Tokyo was like holding an athletics meeting in a sauna. From the spectacular open ceremony, Japan's infamous late-summer humidity inched up toward the truly intolerable mark. The conditions made Liz McColgan's magnificent victory in

match in Lille. The general feeling in Canada was that Johnson had been made a scapegoat for everyone else, that drug taking was rife in athletics and if he had been an American news of his positive drugs test would have been squashed.

done to the sport'. But on others he said, 'The Ben saga has gone on for too long. The press has given the most distress. He's suffered enough.' They had met in Seville at the World Indoor Championships, but Christie dealt easily with Johnson.

The Tokyo race did much to wash away the bad odour that still hung in the air from Seoul. Burrell appeared to be on his way to becoming world champion when he was passed by Lewis at 95 metres. Burrell, who is clinically blind in his right eye, did not see his team-mate pass him. When Lewis thrusts his arms up in the air he has double reason to celebrate. Not only has he won the title for a third successive time (Johnson crossed the line first in 1987 but was retrospectively disqualified) but he had regained his world record. His time was a stunning 9.86 seconds.

Burrell finished second in 9.88, Mitchell third in 9.91 (although it was later claimed he had got a 'flyer', anticipating the gun early and not being recalled for a false start) and Christie fourth in 9.92. The Briton had run a time which if he had

Brothers in arms: Linford and John Regis

Altogether now: Linford leads the singing at the closing ceremony, Split, 1990

But Johnson without his steroids was like popeye without his spinach and his performances had dropped off greatly since 1988 and he had failed to win an individual spot in Canada's team for these Championships.

Christie's views on Johnson varied widely throughout the year of his return. One moment he was claiming he was 'disgusted' with Johnson because 'he has not said sorry for what he has

achieved it two-and-a-half months earlier would have been a world record. Now it was not even good enough to get a medal in the World Championships. In all, six runners broke 10 sec-

onds. Bruny Surin of Canada ran 10.14, which would have won him a silver in the inaugural 1983 Championships – on this occasion it is only good enough for last.

Christie was, understandably, shattered by what had happened. He had run faster than ever but still seemed to be as far away as ever from

'I ran faster than ever before in Tokyo, and I'm still trying to go one better in Barcelona – even the gold '

achieving his ambition of becoming the world's fastest man. In a trackside interview with BBC TV he said he was retiring. And after failing to get through the opening round of the 200 metres the next day, he reiterated that it was all over. 'I don't want to continue running and getting beaten,' he told reporters as he took off his spikes. 'It's better

for me to go out at the top. I am not getting younger and I'm disillusioned.'

While Christie's career seemed dead, Lewis's appeared to have been given the kiss of life. 'The cream of the crop always rises at the big meets,' said Burrell, 'and tonight we saw the cream rise.' Mitchell said: 'Carl proved tonight what he proves every time he gets into the blocks, every time he steps onto a long jump runway, every time he steps on to the track for a relay race – that he's the greatest track athlete ever.'

The 100 metres was considered to be the jewel in the crown of the best athletics meeting ever staged, and Lewis was to be found to the fore in most of the Championships' memorable moments. Mike Powell broke Bob Beamon's legendary world long jump record with a leap of 8.95 metres – Lewis finished second with a wind aided effort of 8.91 – and the United States relay team – anchored by Lewis – set a new world record of 37.50 seconds.

Eighteen months later, however, it was revealed why there had been so many outstanding performances in the explosive events. The track laid at the Olympic Stadium had failed to conform to specifications laid down by the International Amateur Athletic Federation and was too hard, greatly assisting the explosive races like the sprints. But all the world records were allowed to stand. Lewis, naturally, dismissed the claims that he had an unfair advantage. 'There's no such thing as a fast track, only fast people,' he said.

Liz McColgan ended the World Championships as Britain's only individual gold medalholder. But, on the final day, in a brilliant climatic finale inspired by Kriss Akabusi, the 4x400 metres relay team dusted the Americans down the home straight to beat them in a major championship for the first time since the 1936 Olympics. The best other British performance was Sally Gunnell's silver medal in the 400 metres hurdles.

Within two months, Christie had changed his mind about retiring. 'I said I was going to stop, retire there and then,' he said in an interview with *The Voice*. 'I meant it, too. But I got so many letters from people who wanted me to carry on and after having a word with Ron Roddan who said I should give it one more year, I decided to continue.

'If I quit, there'd be no-one else to take my place. Realistically, I could be Europe's number one for the next three or four years. I made that decision to retire because athletics isn't my whole life. It doesn't pay that much and through my other activities I've carved a niche for the future. But after Tokyo, the press were saying, "Wow! He ain't so old".'

He claimed after Tokyo that he had nothing left to prove, but he obviously felt there was, otherwise he would not have reversed his retirement plan. By the turn of 1992, he was acting like his old belligerent self again. 'If someone says I can't run across the road, I'll be damned if I won't prove I can run across that road,' he said. 'They talk all this rubbish about my age and that I should retire. But it doesn't matter to me. I'm still beating all those 21-year-olds – maybe it's them who should retire.

'I feel every year is my year. The Olympic motto is that it's all about the taking part, not the winning, but I believe it's all about the trying. I ran faster than ever before in Tokyo, and I'm still trying to go one better in Barcelona – even the gold.'

To understand what motivates Christie, you have to look back on a life and career during which he has been convinced he has received more than his unfair share of bad luck and racism. He was bullied at school and has suffered maltreatment by the police, ranging from physical violence to being wrongly accused of stealing a car.

In his autobiography, Christie wrote a chilling account of his brush with the law after the Brixton riots when the police went to his home to arrest his brother Russell. 'I was dragged down the hard concrete steps on to the pavement. A policeman kicked my testicles hard. 'This one's for Brixton,' he shouted. I was flung into a police van and Russell was also dragged in.

'He had been handcuffed and was crying with pain, shouting that they were too tight. Blood began to seep from his hands. The policeman who kicked me in the groin began to slap Russell around the head. When I told him to stop

Linford discovers the pain of running 400 metres, GRE British League, 1991

he just laughed. We were taken to the station, dragged to the cells and left there. It was the first time I had ever seen the inside of a police cell. We were in for eight or nine hours but it seemed like days and we felt so helpless, so powerless to right a terrible wrong.'

Christie pleaded not guilty in court but was fined for assault and wilful damage.

There have been other problems with the police down the years, mainly concerning motor cars. The first day he received a new sponsored car the police stopped him four times as he drove through west London. And in 1988, he was arrested at West London Stadium for being in possession of a stolen car. In fact, it had been rented by the British Olympic Association and Christie sued the police, winning £30,000 in damages.

It is perhaps therefore not surprising that Christie sometimes appears to have a chip on his shoulder. 'I know I was born to run,' he said in an interview with Hugh McIlvanney in *The Observer* in 1992, 'because if some other athlete had been forced to put up with everything I've had to put up with, he would have packed it in long ago or been reduced to a total wreck. But all the bad stuff has proved my mental strength. Every time they shit on my head I wear a new hat.'

Comparisons between Christie's treatment can be drawn with that of another former Olympic 100 metres champion, Harold Abrahams, winner of the famous 1924 Chariots of Fire race. Abrahams was a Jew in an era when anti-semitism was rife. He was disliked at Cambridge University where he hired a professional coach, Sam Mussabini, when the Corinthian spirit was supposed to be paramount. One could win, but one mustn't appear to be trying too hard, old chap.

Abrahams overcame all that to carve out a brilliant academic and media career for himself. Christie has said that he does not want to be a role model for black youngsters. He just wants to be a role model for any kid. 'By saying I'm black, I'm limiting my appeal,' he says. 'It means that the white and Asian kids will switch off because they feel I don't belong to them. So I'm not a black role model, but one for all of them.'

As British team captain, Christie loves to wrap himself in the flag. Indeed, at the European Championships in 1986 he did so too literally for the officials' liking. Christie was given a reprimand by Arthur Gold, the British president of the European Athletic Association, for attending the medal ceremony with a Union Jack draped over his shoulders.

And when he returned to Britain sections of the black community rebuked him for being 'too identified with white Britain'. When he was awarded his MBE, Christie also received letters from the same people 'telling me I should turn it down'. He told them, 'I was born in Jamaica but Britain is my home. A lot of people won't agree with me but I'm British through and through. This country gave me the chance and I'm very proud of that. When I run it is 100 per cent for the country and I'm always the first to grab the Union Jack.'

For all his success, however, Christie still suspects that he is not fully appreciated in his adopted land. He is almost paranoid about it. In 1994, he told the French newspaper *L'Equipe*, 'When I win it's "Britain's Linford Christie". But when I lose it's the "Jamaican-born Linford Christie".' In the thousand of press cuttings on Christie, though, you will find no reference to the "Jamaican-born Linford Christie" when he has been beaten.

Fuelling Christie's paranoia, *The Guardian*'s Dave Hill wrote in March 1995, 'Unlike the loveable loser (Frank) Bruno, Christie does not play up to a recognizable British character role. He has captained the British team proudly and waved the Union Jack when he's won. But the biggest public impression is of a fast black man focused totally on his trade. As such, he has yet to be totally embalmed in British popular affection, suggesting that he is deemed, at least, in part an outsider in his own land.'

While not totally eradicated, racism is at least on the decrease in British sport. But in 1993, after Christie's big-money head-to-head against Carl Lewis, the secretary of the Rugby Football Union Dudley Wood showed that racism is not totally dead yet. 'Look at that race between Carl Lewis and Linford Christie at Gateshead,' he said. 'Two of the greatest runners in the world, both black, took £200,000 from the sport and put nothing back. You can see the day when Great Britain stage an athletics match against Kenya – with every athlete black. And who would want to watch then?'

In athletics, thankfully, racism is all but non-existent. The team which represented Britain at the 1993 World Championships in Stuttgart contained 35 black athletes out of a total of 83. 'We only see athletes in the British team,' Christie said. 'If anyone was against black or against white, we would throw them out.'

But when he started being successful he quickly noticed the change in people's attitudes towards him. 'The skinheads don't abuse me,' he admitted on the eve of the 1991 World Championships. 'Now, it's "Hi Linford, how are you doing?" and I can go into shops and take something home without paying for it, just to see if it fits.'

Linford Christie has never lost touch with his Jamaican roots, though. He keeps in touch

(opposite page)
Skeleton figure,
Sheffield, 1991

'A lot of people won't agree with me but I'm British through and through'

culturally with his great love of ragamuffin music. He has even been known to break into a spontaneous recital of his favourite song by Ninjaman during an interview. 'Front teeth, gold teeth, don gorgon. Brush teeth with toothpaste and breath smell sweet 'til Sunday morning, article, don gorgon...' His favourite meal is rices, peas and chicken cooked West Indian style. 'I'm British but you never forget where you were born,' he said.

He extends that to other parts of his life. 'I'm the same person as I was 10, 20 years ago,' he said. 'I've got the same friends I've had from the beginning. I have had a lot of support from my family and friends and they help to keep my feet on the ground. I don't accept that because you get a bit of a celebrity, and the money starts coming in, you have to leave behind the people you knew from the beginning. I believe in remembering that you don't know where you are going but you do know where you are coming from.'

(following pages)
Christie finishes
fourth in the
greatest sprint
race in history
behind Carl
Lewis, who sets
a world record
of 9.86 seconds

bringing home the

Beside the harbour in Barcelona, dominating the Porta de la Paz (Gate of Peace), there is a giant statue of Christopher Columbus, pointing towards the New World. But since Seoul it would have been appropriate if he had turned round and pointed in the opposite direction – towards Montjuic and the Olympic Stadium for the 1992 Games. For four years Spanish gold had been every athlete's dream.

Barcelona is the principal city of Catalonia – 'A separate country within Europe,' declare the full page adverts in the local newspapers. The area is a semi-autonomous province in Spain's north-east corner. Catalonia attempted to secede from Spain in 1714, but was defeated. Barcelona is closer to Marseille, France, than Madrid, Spain's capital. The city is a noisy, vibrant place which maintains a Mediterranean character flavoured with Spanish charm. Some of Spain's most famous artists have been born in Barcelona, including painter Pablo Picasso, sculptor Joan Miró and architect Antonio Gaudi.

Two thousand years old, the city can trace its athletic roots to the second century when a locally born Roman general – Lucius Minicius Natalis Quadronius Verus – won the chariot race in the 227th Olympiad. It had been a long race for Barcelona to get the Olympic Games. It had been trying to get them for more than 70 years. They first bid for the 1924 Games but were turned down. Subsequent efforts in 1936 and 1972 were also unsuccessful. Finally, with the ascent of Barcelona's Juan Antonio Samaranch to president of the International Olympic Committee, the city was awarded the Games.

All summer, Linford Christie's Olympic hopes had been building. They had received their biggest boost, however, not on the European Grand Prix circuit, where he had been winning regularly all season, but on a steamy track in New Orleans thousands of miles away. It was there, sensationally, that Carl Lewis failed to qualify for the United States team. The greatest athlete in history – the 1984 and 1988 Olympic 100 metres champion and 1983, 1987 and 1991 world champion and world record holder – had been knocked out in the US's sudden death first-three-past-the-post, no excuses qualifying system. Out of sorts and out of shape, Lewis could finish only sixth. 'I felt 90 per cent instead of 100 per cent,' he told stunned reporters afterwards. 'I ran the best race I could on this day, but it wasn't good enough. I can accept that.'

Christie was as surprised as everyone else by Lewis's failure but said, 'Every dog has his day, and the Lord now sees fit to let someone else have the rewards.'

Almost overnight, Christie's odds with the bookmakers fell from 50-1 to 12-1. All his career, he had been complaining that the British media did not support him enough, now suddenly when

they did he was having trouble coming to terms with being labelled the favourite.

'The press have been putting pressure on me – but if they really want to help they should put pressure on the Americans. I'm going out there to do my best – but nothing's guaranteed. There are still three good Americans to beat. Leroy Burrell, Dennis Mitchell and Mark Witherspoon are very fast. There are a couple of good Nigerians who have run under ten seconds as well. But I've got to be positive about winning a medal.'

since he won the European Indoor 60 metres title earlier in the year, had failed an out-of-competition drugs test in England and was to be sent home. The pressure on Christie was already huge and, as he counselled Livingston well into the evening, this threatened to send him over the edge as he was sucked into the whole affair. In his agitated state of mind, he shouted at photographers taking pictures of him and screwed up a reporter's notebook. A sense of Olympic *déjà vu* must have washed over Christie.

While Olympic fervour was growing back home, Christie headed to the sun-kissed, gamblers' playground of Monte Carlo to finish his preparations. 'I'm going to be tip-toeing through the tulips,' he said, 'sharpening my speed, relaxing a bit and having a laugh. Come the race I'll be ready. If I'm relaxed on the starting line I'll do the business. But I don't want that I "gotta win, I gotta win" feeling in my head.'

However, all those carefully laid preparations were disrupted when disaster struck on the eve of his opening heat. It was announced that Jason Livingston, a young training partner of Christie's who had been tipped to fill the big man's shoes

Back in Britain, Livingston's disgrace was the main news item on the evening news and filled pages and pages of the next day's newspapers. But since Ben Johnson, sprinters and drugs have, unfortunately, become wedded. In the open court of who takes what and when and where, accusations fly frequently. It is therefore ironic that Livingston should have revelled in the nickname 'Baby Ben' because he shared the same stature as Johnson, had his hair shaved like Johnson and even wore the same brand of running spikes as Johnson. But this was taking hero worship a step too far, surely.

Unfortunately, because he has been able to

continue running so quickly in his 30s Christie inevitably also draws his fair share of suspicion in this whispering campaign. Despite the tough anti-drugs stance he had always adopted, this latest episode did nothing to dampen the rumours. But there has never been any evidence that Christie has used anything stronger than an aspirin (or ginseng). In 1994, he took 16 random drugs tests and passed every one.

In an interview with France's *L'Equipe* magazine after the Olympics, Christie said, 'The world

illusions. They can't understand how you do it and tell themselves something is up. It's the easiest way to explain to themselves why they are losing.'

It was a relief for Christie to step on the track and begin competing on the first day of the Olympic track and field programme. This was a world he knew. The press could not touch him out here. Yet even here there was still the smell of a drugs cheat in the air when the biggest cheers were awarded to Ben Johnson, making a return to

of athletics has gone mad. Everyone thinks everyone is taking drugs. We'll see about that when drugs tests are introduced. When I was suspected of taking ephedrine in Seoul, I said to myself: "My God, I now understand how these things can happen." '

After the women's Olympic 100 metres final, American Gwen Torrence publicly accused two of the three women ahead of her of using performance enhancing drugs. 'You'll never hear me saying so-and-so is taking drugs,' said Christie. 'If people admit it, it must be so. But if they deny it, I won't make the least comment. When you beat some people all the time, they have these

Olympic competition. It was a cruel twist of fate that while Carl Lewis, the man who had been cheated out of Olympic glory four years earlier, was not allowed to run, Ben Johnson, the biggest cheat in Olympic history, was.

Christie's victory in his first round heat was an untroubled affair. In the second round later on in the day he was drawn against Johnson and Leroy Burrell. Burrell had beaten Christie in their last ten meetings and when he had been asked by a British journalist at a pre-Olympic press conference whether he considered Linford Christie a big threat had answered, 'Do you seriously expect me to say yes?'

The best in the world: Olympic 100 metre champion

(opposite) Linford hits back at his critics after his victory

There were three false starts, the last of them down to Johnson. He waved his arms about in a theatrical manner and stared at the starter in protest, albeit to no effect. It was a strange sight to see this former battleship of a man reduced to the runt the Good Lord meant him to be standing next to Christie, who stood a statuesque 6 foot 2 inches and rippled with muscles. When they finally got away, it was clear how powerless Johnson had become without artificial aids to help him along. He got away sharply but within 20 metres the race was between Christie and Burrell. It looked as if Christie was keen to score a psychological point over his American rival because he pulled away from him to win in 10.07 seconds. Without hesitating, Christie was down the tunnel not sparing a glance at either Burrell or Johnson. It was only Burrell's second defeat in 21 races and he admitted, 'Linford's looking good'.

In the next day's semi-finals, Burrell tried desperately to regain that edge by shadowing Christie 9.97 to 10.00 seconds. But it was the end of the road for Ben Johnson. He finished last, giving up when he quickly realized he was not going to qualify for the final. 'I tried my best, what more can I say?' he shrugged. As he bent down to collect his kit, Christie gave him a consoling pat on the shoulder. Seven months later Johnson failed another drugs test and was kicked out of the sport for life.

In the other semi-final, Mark Witherspoon, a man Carl Lewis had been tipping for great things, was cruelly cut down by an achilles tendon injury. He lasted just a few strides before slumping to the track in agony. Christie admitted later that when he went to Barcelona, he was 90 per cent sure of winning. After the semi-finals, he was certain he was going to win.

In the run-up to the Olympics, Christie had made a small but vital change which he believed made all the difference to his chances. For most of his career, he has relied on his incredible mid-race surge to carry him to victory. His quickness out of the starting blocks had been limited. Indeed, in many of his races he had been sluggish. This always gave his opponents hope that if they could react really quickly to the gun – as Dennis Mitchell had done in Tokyo the previous year – they would gain a vital metre's advantage over Christie.

In a race lasting ten seconds that might as well be a mile at the top level. But Malcolm Arnold, one of the most technically gifted coaches in the world and Colin Jackson's personal trainer, had made a suggestion. Why not adjust his block settings to those used by Jackson? Christie had followed the advice, and was now starting faster than at any other time in his career. Researchers at Crewe And Alsager College estimated that Christie produced a force of 1,800 newtons when he left his blocks in Barcelona – that is the same power needed to accelerate a Ford Fiesta from nought to 60 in 10.4 seconds.

The eight finalists settled into their blocks 15 minutes after Gail Devers had completed one of the most remarkable comebacks in Olympic history by winning the women's 100 metres. Two years earlier the American could not walk and faced having her feet amputated after doctors diagnosed a serious thyroid condition.

Like Christie, Leroy Burrell had tried to gain every possible legal advantage for the biggest race of his career. He was wearing a new pair of state-of-the-art spikes manufactured by Japanese firm Asics, their spikes angled at 105 degrees to push against the track at the most effective angle. But the one thing he could not totally control was his nerves. A barely perceptible twitch in the blocks triggered a forward lunge by Christie and a false start. Then, on the second attempt, Dennis Mitchell signalled he was unhappy with the noise made by the stadium's 64,800 capacity crowd, raised his hand and the start was aborted.

Christie, though, was totally composed throughout. He stood perfectly still, his left leg placed slightly in front of his right, his arms loose, his eyes fixed on some far and glorious horizon, never blinking. The concentration was

immense, his presence huge. A troupe of dancing girls or a pack of man-eating lions could have been standing in the lane next to him and he would not have flickered.

'I was focused down the line,' he explained. 'I wasn't looking for anybody else. I wasn't taking any prisoners. I was just concentrating on my own lane and getting to the other end as fast as I could. Really, I can't remember much about it.'

Christie, who had taught himself to concentrate so deeply after watching a German sprinter use it in 1986, explained, 'It's like being in a little coma. I'm not aware of the crowd or any of my opponents. It's just me. In the past I've worried about what was happening on either side and I have run tight. I used to run on aggression, but now I have learned that it is the man who stays relaxed the longest who wins the race.'

Christie, benefiting from the change Arnold had suggested, got away smartly and began his familiar, fists-punching-the air rush almost immediately. At 20 metres he was third behind Frankie Fredericks of Namibia and Bruny Surin of Canada. But by 40 metres he was level with his rivals, when so often in the past he had still been behind. Then at 60 metres he burst away. Fredericks and Mitchell tried desperately to stay with him but this was Christie's day. He took just 45 strides to win in 9.96 seconds, six-hundredths of a second ahead of Fredericks. It was not just a gloriously famous victory, it was a magnificent rout. The medal Daley Thompson always called the 'Big G' had surely never been won with such style.

At 32, Christie had become the oldest man to win the blue riband event of the Olympic Games. He was four years older than Allan Wells had been when he won in Moscow in 1980. But not since Harold Abrahams's 'Chariots of Fire' win in Paris in 1924 had a Briton managed to beat the Americans in the Olympic 100 metres – the United States had boycotted Moscow. 'It's about time someone other than the Americans won this title,' said Christie.

'They told me I was too old, and old men don't win the sprints, but Linford Christie never accepted that. I'm glad I gave up those nights in the discotheque. It's got to be the greatest moment of my life ... and now I'm going out and celebrating,' Christie said after completing a lap

of honour draped, inevitably, in the Union Jack.

'Colin Jackson, who I'm sharing a room with, said: "You ain't coming back here with anything other than the gold medal. This is the gold medal room."'

Sadly, Jackson's own Olympics were to quickly turn into a nightmare when he could finish only seventh in his 110 metres hurdles final – an event he was considered the odds-on favourite for.

'It's always been my ambition to be number one in the world. It's taken a long time, it's been

'I won by this much'

We did it: Christie is embraced by young team-mate, triple jumper Julian Golley

Christie wins at the Les Jones Memorial Games, Belfast, 1992

(opposite)
Contented

a slow process – and I'm clean. The Olympics is the pinnacle of every athlete's career. At 32, they said I was too old – but I did it. I have been going to championships since 1986 and it's still great to hear "God Save the Queen".'

Telegrams flooded in for Christie, including one from Allan Wells. The two had not always enjoyed the cosiest of relationships but one great champion could still honour another. 'I felt if I'd been through the wringer again,' said Wells from his Guildford home, 'partly because I wanted him to win and partly because of the distinct memories of Moscow it brought back. They can hang other gold medals around your neck at Commonwealth and European championships but there is nothing to compare with an Olympic gold.'

Christie returned to a standing ovation at the

(opposite)
Linford Christie:
a sprinter
who has never
thrown the
towel in

athletes' village. He showed his medal to his team-mates and then dropped it casually into his kit bag. 'I've got to put it behind me,' he told them. 'There are other challenges ahead.'

Across the Atlantic – where track and field

or titanium medal. I'm proud of myself so Americans should be proud of me.'

But the American media were beginning to ask, 'Now what would have happened if Carl Lewis had been there...'

Christie replied, 'Carl Lewis wasn't here today but he can't go on forever. It's my day today.'

Almost as soon as Christie crossed the line in Barcelona, the spotlight fell on the race for another kind of Olympic gold: money. An Olympic gold medal in the right event is the most valuable marketing tool to own in sport. It's not the winning, it's the taking part philosophy – that is for losers. Christie was a winner and there was now a pot of gold waiting

'It's always been my ambition to be number one in the world. It's taken a long time, it's been a slow process – and I'm clean'

ranks below tractor pulling for popularity except in Olympic year when it suddenly assumes great importance – there was considerable debate as to how America had lost the 100 metres to a limey, especially after their 1-2-3 of the previous year in Tokyo. It was an event they considered their own. Dennis Mitchell, far from being praised for his bronze medal was criticized. In the end, exasperated, he said, 'Sprinting is a very intricate thing and people have to understand that. Americans can't win everything all of the time. I will wear my medal as proudly as if it were a gold, platinum

for him at the end of the rainbow. Many people still labour under the misapprehension that the Olympics is for amateurs, but every dollar and cent Christie earned out of his run in Barcelona was perfectly legal.

That is because the word 'amateur' had been struck from the Olympic charter in 1981. The International Olympic Committee turned over eligibility rules to the individual sports federations in 1987. Athletics had effectively gone open in 1984 when the International Amateur Athletic Federation (to this day the Amateur in the IAAF

Smelling
of roses: yet
another victory
lap for Linford,
Les Jones
Memorial
Games, Belfast,
1992

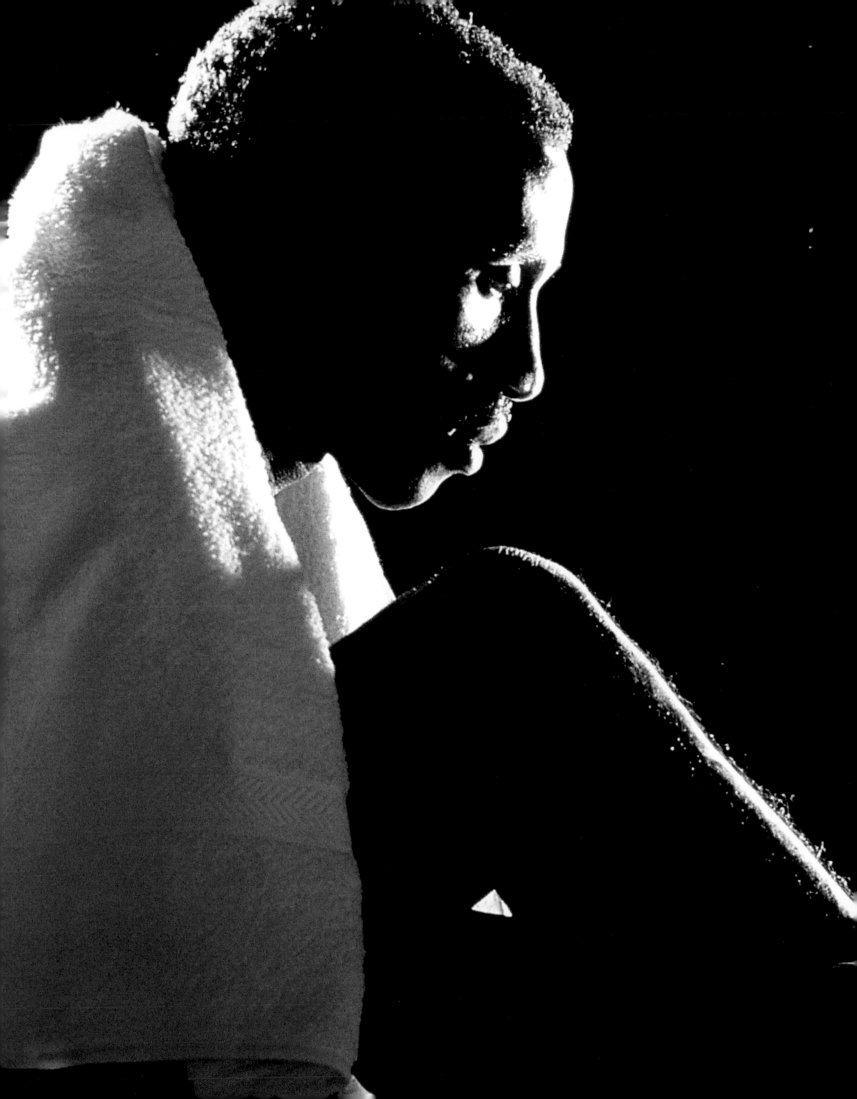

The man to put
your shirt on,
Barcelona, 1992

survives) had invented trust funds. Competitors could receive appearance money and endorsement contracts, but the money had to be deposited in trust funds. Funds for expenses could be drawn out and the whole amount could be cashed upon retirement. It was effectively a fig leaf for amateurism.

Athletes had been making money out of the Olympics long before amateurism was officially abolished. In 1976, Bruce Jenner had made £3 million out of his victory in the decathlon by appearing on everything from Wheaties boxes to TV sitcoms.

Christie's Olympic victory catapulted him instantly on to millionaires' row. Overnight, his appearance fee on the European grand prix circuit rocketed from £15,000 per race to £25,000. He received a gold medal bonus of £50,000 from Puma, his personal kit wear sponsors. In addition, when he came to negotiate his next contract with Puma his annual retainer shot up to £120,000. Lucrative sponsorship deals with soft drinks manufacturer Lucozade, men's clothing company High & Mighty and The Banana Group were all to follow in the next 18 months.

In October, to cash in on his new earning potential, Christie set up a promotions company based in Richmond – with Colin Jackson – called Nuff Respect. 'I knew by becoming Olympic champion I would be opening new doors and realized that I needed someone to look after the opportunities that would come my way in the media, endorsements and sponsorship,' he said.

In a survey in *Business Age* magazine in April 1994, Christie's total wealth was estimated at £3.10 million. However, that still made him only the 34th highest earning sportsman in Britain behind the likes of motor racing driver Nigel Mansell (£45 million), golfer Nick Faldo (£35 million), snooker player Steve Davies (£8.50 million), footballer John Fashanu (£4 million) and ice skater Robin Cousins (£3.50 million).

Christie was not even the wealthiest athlete: Daley Thompson had £3.20 million. Other athletes in the survey included Sebastian Coe (£3 million), Alan Pascoe (£2 million), Geoff Capes (£1.30 million), Steve Ovett (£1.25 million), Colin Jackson (£1.20 million), Steve Cram (£1.10 million), Fatima Whitbread (£1.10 million) and Tessa Sanderson (£1 million).

Following his victory in the 100 metres, Christie was deflated, which was hardly surprising after scaling such a massive peak. He was knocked out in the semi-finals of the 200 metres. But as the end of the Games approached, there was a touching moment, which displayed a side to Christie the public rarely get to hear about. Earlier in the summer Christie had threatened to 'deck' one of Britain's leading 400 metres runners after having criticized the 4x400 metres relay which had won the world title in 1991, for what he believed to be an over-exuberant attitude since then.

When the two athletes met in Barcelona they did not come to blows, but instead hugged each other. It was just minutes after Christie had watched the brave Derek Redmond complete his semi-final of the 400 metres on one leg after pulling a hamstring. Redmond was hobbling to catch a bus to take him back to the athletes village when he met Christie. 'He came over and put his arms out and we just embraced,' recalled Redmond. 'Linford's a big softie really, though he'll kill me for saying that.'

When he returned back from Barcelona, Christie went home to Thornfield Road, Shepherd's Bush, to show off his medal to his family. He had already received an emotional welcome at Heathrow Airport. 'Everything stopped dead. It was like it used to be for the Beatles,' said a policeman who was on duty. Among the people to meet him there was his mother, Mabel, still struggling after a stroke and sitting in a wheelchair. He hung the medal round her neck and said, 'This is for you.' It was another touching moment.

Back in west London, everyone wanted to touch the medal, shake Linford's hand. 'You've got to realize how it was at the start,' he said. 'These are the people who were around and were encouraging me the most. What you are looking at now is ten years of hard work, not ten seconds.'

A neighbour asked him how it felt. 'Shall, I tell you, the winning of it was a bit of an anticlimax,' he said. 'There's all those years of hard work you put in and then there's the race and it's all over in seconds. Today I'm here with my family, tomorrow I'm back training again because I'm running in Sheffield on Friday.'

Even with the Big G against your name, life goes on.

CHAPTER 5

Andy Norman was driving along the M25 in his Mercedes when he took a call on his car telephone. The Mr Fix-it of British athletics spoke to the caller from California for a few minutes. When he hung up he had struck a deal to stage the richest race in athletics history.

'Anything superman can do ...'

Joe Douglas, the pint-sized manager of Carl Lewis, and Norman, the former police sergeant who controlled Linford Christie's career, had finally reached an agreement for their two men to get together to determine who was the fastest man in the world. Ever since the Barcelona Olympics, Lewis had been making noises about a big head-to-head showdown.

At one stage it appeared the re-match might take place in the car park of a Las Vegas hotel in May 1993 in a packaged-for-television competition. That would have netted Christie a cool $250,000 share of a total prize fund of $1 million. Lewis, who was also to have long jumped against world champion and record holder Mike Powell, was due to collect $500,000. But the scheme foundered on financial difficulties with Home Box Office, the American cable television company who have promoted so many boxing world title fights. Then subsequent moves to stage the race in Crystal Palace and Birmingham also failed.

By this time, Lewis was growing impatient at waiting for his opportunity. 'He is more inventive than Ben Johnson was in going out of his way to avoid me,' said the American. Christie was livid when the quote was relayed to him and retorted, 'I may be annoyed enough to meet Carl before the World Championships in Stuttgart.'

Finally, with Zurich ready to open their cheque book to secure the race, Douglas and Norman agreed that the two sprinters would share £200,000 for their appearance at the Vauxhall International in Gateshead on 11 July, making the event even bigger than Zola Budd's £90,000 re-match with Mary Decker-Slaney at Crystal Palace in 1985. 'I guess Linford has finally caved into the pressure,' said a satisfied Lewis. 'It's going to be good for the sport that we are able to compete. But there was no reason to have taken this long. I feel very confident that I can win.'

Gateshead, Christie's favourite stadium, was a strange place to hold this latest sprint 'race of the century'. While some of the major stadiums in Europe had been prepared to stage the event, the International Stadium is a modest 11,500 seater arena. This Friday, as usual, there was a strong wind whipping off the River Tyne and the temperature of 66ºF was nearly 30º below what Lewis has been training in every day in his home city of Houston. A few minutes before the off, there was also a light north-east drizzle, which thankfully eased off in time for the race. It must have all

seemed very surreal to Lewis, who had arrived only the previous evening on a Concorde flight.

In contrast to Christie, who had been keeping a low profile all week, Lewis once again proved himself to be the master of hype. He was talking a good race at least. 'He's never beaten me in a major championships,' he said. 'And there is no way I wouldn't have won gold in Barcelona. The monster is awakening. I'm in the best shape of my life and will be strong – very strong – when I line up against Linford.'

Christie had been maintaining since the match had been made that he was not staking his entire season on the race. 'I'm not training especially for this,' he insisted. 'The World Championships in a few weeks are my main target. This is just another race. But I think I'm going to win. If I thought I wasn't, I wouldn't go.

'Lewis didn't make the Olympics. He wasn't good enough to make the American team and kept saying I only won because he wasn't there. That annoyed me a little bit. Lewis has tried to have a go at me but I'm not getting involved in that. I'm waiting until the end of the race and maybe after I have won I will reply to him.'

Far more contentious were Christie's remarks about the size of his purse. 'Lennox Lewis and Frank Bruno are receiving £5 million for their fight,' he pointed out. 'They get bruised faces, I know that. But I can pull muscles. I don't think I'm getting paid enough to be honest with you.'

Indeed, there was considerable debate about

Celebrating
with the family:
Linford is
embraced by
his father James
after his win

(opposite)
'I'm No. 1'

wiched between the little men Jon Drummond and André Cason, Burrell powered to victory in 10.02 seconds. He beat Christie by the narrowest of margins, one-hundredth of a second, although the Briton's time was his best of the season. Suddenly, though, the media and American sprinters, were beginning raising doubts again about whether Christie really was the world number one.

'I thought I had it won,' admitted Christie. But as soon as he saw Burrell celebrating he knew he was wrong. 'This was my World Championships,' said the American. 'I had to win this one.' Consolation for Christie came in the fact that Lewis was beaten again; he finished fourth. 'I was watching Drummond and Cason,' explained Christie. 'But I'm still very happy. It's my fastest time of the year.'

Twelve days later, after Linford Christie had uppercut the darkening skies and fired imaginary bullets at British fans to show he was the 'Top

Gun' after his 100 metres victory at the World Championships in Stuttgart, it was easy to forget that so much had ever been made of Christie's defeat in Zurich. Because now in three swift preliminaries and one awesome final those Americans who believed he was a 'king without a crown' would need to search for evidence in some other venue rather than the Gottlieb Daimler Stadium.

Of all the individual events the 100 metres can often be the most difficult to predict. After all, it's just ten seconds of running. Proper execution allows no margin for error, and Zurich had demonstrated that even one mistake can tip the balance of a race. Assessing great sprinters as they run the preliminaries is a dangerous exercise, rather like judging racehorses as they walk round the parade ring. Still, all eyes were trained on the sprinters as they took their blocks for the event's first round on Saturday, 14 August, the opening day of the Championships. In his heat, Christie languished in mid-pack for the first few strides of the race before easing away for a comfortable victory in 10.24 seconds.

Others were not quite so lackadaisical about round one. André Cason and Carl Lewis turned in the two fastest times of the round, Cason popping an eye-opening 10.08 and Lewis, shutting down his engines five metres before the end and still finishing in 10.15. Clearly, the Americans were determined to back up all their words with action. 'I'm not trying to run fast,' says Cason as he stepped off the track. 'I'm just doing what I've been taught.'

In round two, while Christie waited his turn, Lewis cracked another impressive performance and blasted a 10.11, while Dennis Mitchell also looked good with a 10.08. It is as if the two were parked and tooting their horns in front of Christie's house. C'mon out, Linford!

And come he did. In the third heat of round two, after watching Lewis and Mitchell have their moments of fleeting glory, Christie roared back and stopped the clock dead on 10 seconds, his fastest time since he won the Olympic title in Barcelona. But even Christie was upstaged by Cason in the final heat. The short, heavily muscled 24-year-old from Virginia Beach ran four-hundredths of a second quicker, and his 9.96 was the fastest time in the world in 1993. Did it mean he had the psychological edge over Christie? 'No, I don't. Tomorrow's a new day. That's all you can say.' The day had been one of compelling gladiatorial combat which had kept the crowd on the edge of their seats.

The first semi-final on Sunday featured both Cason and Lewis, as well as Nigeria's Daniel Effiong, a man some people were tipping to spring a surprise. But Lewis seemed to have trouble staying with the pace, and by 30 metres was well adrift of the action as Cason cruised to a wind-assisted victory in 9.94 seconds. Lewis salvaged third place with 9.98. The years were clearly catching up with his 32-year-old body. In the second semi, Christie got a good start and won easily in 9.97. The stage was set for the final.

The two hours between the semi-final and final are always a nervous time, when seconds seem like minutes and minutes seem like hours. The energy squandered during this period while they are forced to wait can cost athletes titles.

Each had developed their own little routine to while away the time as they scattered around the warm-up area. Christie sat alone; Lewis flopped back on a high jump mat and closed his eyes; Mitchell had his shoulders massaged; and Cason sat with his coach, Loren Seagrave, working out how he could win.

When it was time for the sprinters to go to their blocks everything was still. The flags of the 183 nations taking part in these Championships hung limp around the Stadium originally built by Adolf Hitler. At this moment it was possible to believe that the world had stopped spinning for a moment. The pistol shot which cracked around the silent stadium set the sprinters on their way. Mitchell, just as he had been in Tokyo two years earlier, was the first to react. But then, incredibly, only a couple of thousandths of a second behind was Linford Christie.

Every sprinter decelerates during the last 30 or 40 metres of the 100, and it is generally accepted that the winner is the one who decelerates the slowest. But whether it is the bio-mechanics of Christie's 6 foot 2 inch frame which allowed him to accelerate mid-race better than his rivals and hold on to that burst longer, we do not know. At top speed, statistics show he covered the ground in Stuttgart at 27 miles per hour. When you add the 'best start of my career' on top of that equation you come up with as near the perfect

sprinting performance as you can hope to see.

In this split second it had taken Christie to raise from his blocks the rest of the world was beaten. By 15 metres he was ahead, his head still, his arms pumping, eating up the ground underneath him. Cason came up briefly to challenge him, but it was never a serious threat. As the line approached, Christie widened his arms in a grand gesture of victory while those behind stretched and grimaced in defeat. For a moment, the clock was forgotten. But then when Christie saw the time of '9.87' a huge smile broke out across his face. 'I thought 9.90 was possible, but 9.87...' said Christie, his voice trailing off. It did not matter that he had missed the world record by just one-hundredth of a second.

'This is even better than winning the Olympics because everyone was here,' he said pointedly, referring to Lewis's absence in Barcelona. 'All the guys were here, the big men, no-one was missing. No arguments.'

Lewis, dejected, hollow-eyed, after finishing fourth in 10.02 as Cason in 9.92 and Mitchell in 9.99 took the silver and bronze medals, was magnanimous in defeat. 'Linford ran an incredible race,' he told American television. 'It's nice to see him win because he deserves it. He was the hungriest person in the world this year.'

Past differences were forgotten all round, if only temporarily. 'It was an act of genius, the master craftsman at his best,' said Frank Dick, the British chief coach who Christie had come to blows with in the past. 'The better man on the day won,' conceded Cason. Christie even had a good word to say about his bitterest rival, claiming: 'Carl Lewis is still the greatest athlete of all time but now I should be up there with him somewhere.' On this night, Linford Christie had everybody's respect and looked at peace with himself.

There was an added bonus for Christie. No £100,000 pay-cheque this time but instead a brand new Mercedes car. The automobiles were being awarded to all the champions in Stuttgart. It was the International Amateur Athletic Federation's answer to criticism that there was no prize money at these World Championships. Ironically, Christie already owned a Mercedes ('a bigger one than they're giving me here'). At the medal ceremony he was presented with a model one and accepted it graciously. But as soon as the

athletes disappeared from the view of the crowd an official from the IAAF took it back to be presented to the next world champion!

Christie's performance – he also helped the 4x100 metres relay team to the silver medals behind the Americans – was the highlight of Britain's best ever World Championships. There were also gold medals for Christie's great friend and training partner Colin Jackson, in the 110 metres hurdles, and Sally Gunnell, in the 400 metres hurdles. When Christie and Gunnell arrived home at Heathrow Airport's Terminal One they were accorded the reception normally reserved for film stars or pop groups. One flag declared, 'Champions!' Another banner boasted, 'Biggest, Baddest, Best ... and British!'

Twenty minutes after touching down, Christie and Gunnell gave a press conference. 'I think it's about time we got the credit we deserve,' said Christie. 'We are doing better than the footballers, better than the rugby players, better than the cricketers. We don't get enough coverage. There were more pages written about my lunch box than my win. When am I going to get some credit, some respect? It would be nice to

Captain Courageous: World Cup, Havana, 1993

be taken seriously.'

In the year since his victory in the Barcelona Olympics, Christie had become increasingly annoyed about the 'Lunch box' jibes. The phase had been coined by – who else? – the *Sun*. 'Linford Christie is way out in front in every department – and we don't just mean the way he stormed to victory in the 100 metres,' started an article a few days after his victory. 'His skin-tight lycra shorts hide little as he pounds down the track and his Olympic sized talents are a source of delight for women around the world.' They then had a picture of a black model with several suggestions as to what could be stuck down the front of his shorts 'to achieve that Linford look'. They included a king-size Mars bar and a medium cucumber from Tesco.

It was easy to understand why Christie felt so upset. He has just achieved the greatest victory of his career and is being lauded around the world. Yet, back home in the country he was representing, the most popular newspaper was full of speculation about how big his genitals are. It was racial stereotyping of the worst type. 'Imagine if people made similar remarks about Sally Gunnell's tits,' he told one interviewer.

His anger was increased the day after his victory over Carl Lewis in Gateshead when there was an advert for Heineken in the newspapers. Above their slogan, '...refreshes the parts other beers cannot reach', stood a spindly athletic specimen. The second photograph showed him drinking a can of lager. In the third he was transformed, revealing more a Harrods hamper than a lunch box. However, Christie himself is not above cashing in on his famous 'Lunch box'. In 1994, he signed an advertising deal with The Banana Group to promote bananas: the slogan, 'Power Pack Eating with Linford', and all the photographs used to promote the campaign were a clear play on 'Linford's Lunch box'.

Christie craves respect more than anything else, but just when he is on the point of earning it he does something which means it is denied to him. Like decathlete Daley Thompson, Christie has a self-destruct button which he seems to push at every opportunity he gets. An example came in Stuttgart. An hour after running the greatest race of his career, Christie was sitting in the winner's press conference held in a temporary marquee

The ultimate accolade: BBC Sports Personality of the Year 1993, with runners-up Nigel Mansell and Sally Gunnell

behind the main stand. The conference was winding up when a German reporter asked him a question. 'Did you get a personal reaction from Carl Lewis?' he said. Christie did not understand, or did not want to understand, the question. The reporter asked again. 'Do you have a personal relationship with Carl Lewis?'

Christie sighed. He was bored with the press conference, but rather than answer the question politely, he said: 'Yeah. He's kissing me on the lips every night.' Cason and Mitchell, who were sitting either side of Christie, at first tittered then looked downwards, clearly embarrassed. Because of his dislike of the press, Christie once again presented the wrong image to the media when the eyes of the world were upon him.

Christie's lust for appreciation is why the BBC TV Sports Personality of the Year Award is so important to him. The prize is the most valued of the many awards which are presented to sports-

men and woman each year, the Grand Daddy of them all. The list of winners reads like a who's who of British sport: Chris Chataway, Bobby Moore, Henry Cooper, Princess Anne, John Curry, Virginia Wade, Ian Botham, Torvill and Dean, Nick Faldo and Paul Gascoigne.

Christie should have won the Award after his Olympic victory, but astonishingly was overlooked in favour of motor racing driver Nigel Mansell. That defeat probably rankled more with Christie than any he has suffered on the track. But when he heard he had won the 1993 Award he was willing to fly back from his winter training base in Australia for the weekend to collect it. 'It shows people appreciate what you are doing,' he said. 'That's why you compete, for the recognition, because you are a showman. I don't compete just for my own satisfaction, or else I might as well run behind closed doors. An award like that is worth more to me than money.'

Showing w

No.1

Zurich is the richest, most prestigious event on the international Grand Prix circuit. In the one year in four there is no Olympic Games or World Championships, the Weltklasse meeting stands as the peak for many athletes. Indeed, its quality is so high that Zurich has been dubbed 'The Seven-hour Olympics'.

Yet in many ways it is tougher for Christie to win here than at the Olympics or World Championships because there are ten Americans allowed to run, not just three. For 1994, Andres Brugger, the meeting promoter, loosened his purse strings more than ever to purchase the finest sprint talent on earth. It cost him £250,000 to gather together the best field of the year. It was the most expensively assembled race in history in the richest athletics meeting in history.

Mirror image

He brought not only Christie but also Leroy Burrell, who earlier in the summer had stunned the sport by setting a new world record of 9.85 seconds the day after stepping off a plane in Lausanne, Dennis Mitchell, the Goodwill Games champion who had broken ten seconds five times already during the season, and assorted other world class American sprinters who all believed they were the greatest thing since sliced bread – and were not afraid of saying so to anyone who would listen.

'Mentally, it's very taxing,' said Christie when asked about taking on this battalion of Americans. 'Because at the end of the day, no matter how many athletes have broken 10 seconds or set world records, I am The Guy out there. I'm the Olympic champion, I'm always the only European going against four or five Americans. It's like me versus all the rest. And it's very, very lonely.'

world number one. He was particularly upset over an incident earlier during the summer at the Goodwill Games in St Petersburg, an event which he had been forced to miss after pulling up with a hamstring injury in the Grand Prix meeting at Crystal Palace. Carl Lewis and Burrell were being interviewed at a press conference when they were asked a question about Christie. In an obviously rehearsed answer, they replied, 'Linford Who?'

(facing page)
Linford relaxing

Sprinters are the sport's gladiators. As well as the essential fast-twitch fibres, raw power and a will to win, there is another quality that oozes from the imposing and highly muscled athletes who now dominate the line-up of all championship sprint finals – a touch of arrogance. The Americans seem to learn it at prep school, but it had taken Linford Christie a few years to develop it. But now he has discovered it, he almost reeks of arrogance.

And after his Barcelona and Stuttgart performances, he had every right to splash it all over himself. He remained angry because the Americans still refused to acknowledge him as the

Christie was sandwiched between two championships. He had arrived in Zurich from the European Championships in Helsinki and at the end of the week he was due to fly to Victoria, Canada, for the Commonwealth Games.

But the Zurich meeting had been the main focus of his season and he was approaching it as though it were the Olympic Games or World Championships. 'This will be tougher than the Olympics,' he predicted.

Christie was coming off a mixed European Championships. He had won the 100 metres title for the third successive time, equalling the record of the great Soviet sprinter Valeri Borzov, but had

Hat-trick: Christie wins his third successive European 100 metres title in Helsinki, 1994, from team-mate Jason John (no. 429), Aleksandr Porkhomovskiy of Russia (761) and Mark Blume of Germany (463)

been a frustrated spectator on the last leg as he saw another certain gold medal snatched from his grasp when Darren Braithwaite dropped the baton in the semi-final of the 4x100 metres relay. He also came under fire from Peter Radford, the chief executive of the British Athletic Federation, for two 'ill-advised' pieces of behaviour. They were pulling on a sponsor's T-shirt that read '3x gold, 3x these shoes' during his lap of honour after the 100 metres and for crossing the arena to talk to Dalton Grant while the high jump was still in progress.

It was not the first time Christie's conduct has not been befitting that of the British team captain. On one occasion in the press room in Birmingham he had grabbed Martin Gillingham, a former international team-mate turned journalist with *Athletics Today* magazine, by the throat and pinned him up against the wall because he claimed he had written something he did not like. At Zurich in 1993, he had used threatening and abusive behaviour towards Simon Greenberg, the athletics correspondent of the *Mail on Sunday*, in front of three young members of the British team and a woman team member.

In many ways, Christie has become bigger than British athletics since his victory in Barcelona. He is the captain of the country's most successful team, and there is no doubt his feats have made him a national hero who transcends his sporting arena, but he appears to exert too much influence and believe that he is above the rules which bind everyone else, a view reinforced by the fact that the British Athletic Federation refuse to impose on him even the mildest form of disciplinary action when he steps out of line.

The T-shirt incident was a classic case. As official kit suppliers to British Athletics, View From have paid a lot of money to see stars like Christie, Colin Jackson and Sally Gunnell wear vests bearing their logo. Why should Puma, Christie's personal sponsors, be allowed to ambush that deal and have free exposure? It merely underlined the fact that Christie's captaincy has always been more impressive in terms of personal performance than by any moral leadership he has shown.

Christie had also astonished row-upon-row of representatives of the foreign media in Helsinki when, just moments after winning his 100 metres

title, he strode purposefully towards the press benches, eyes ablaze with anger, to seek out David Moore of the *Daily Mirror*. 'Why do you write such shit?' he shouted at Moore. 'You know it's not true.' British journalists were used to having copies of their articles waved under their noses by an angry Christie, but even they were surprised when he did it minutes after winning a major championship title.

But on this occasion the media could enjoy Zurich. Christie was once again in a snarling, aggressive mood, but it was the Americans who he was angry at. 'If they want to regard me as the underdog that's fine,' he barked. 'I can come round the back and snatch the bone away from them. Pound for pound I'm stronger than the Americans.' He was, in American parlance, ready to kick some butt.

Christie, however, continues to fail to understand why people keep saying he is powered by anger and frustration. 'Often I don't recognize the man called Linford Christie who I read about in

the papers,' he claims. 'Maybe those writers think that because I am big and strong, I must be aggressive too. But that isn't the me I know.'

Not all his rivals can claim to be so placid, however. By the end of the week Zurich, with its brilliant collection of athletic performances, was making headlines around the world for absolutely the wrong reasons. All the ill-feeling that had been bubbling away under the surface of the sprint world for several years, spilled out violently in a few seconds of madness. At 2 a.m. the morning after the race, Dennis Mitchell allegedly kicked Olapde Adeniken in the head while the Nigerian was pinned to the hotel lobby carpet by two other men. Adeniken, one of Christie's biggest rivals for the Commonwealth title, was so badly hurt that he had to withdraw injured from the next Grand Prix meeting in Brussels.

'Some sprinters are very aggressive people,' Christie told *Sports Illustrated* magazine when asked about the incident. 'Hurdlers, for example, can talk to each other; sprinters cannot. Hurdlers go against barriers, but sprinters go against each other. Of course, even in such an environment you should always be in control. It's a shame this happened.'

But that was all to come later. On the eve of the race, when Christie heard that Lewis, who has not been a true force anyway since his victory at Tokyo in 1991 despite all the hype, had withdrawn from Zurich because of a stomach infection he picked up in St Petersburg, Christie was angry. 'Sick? Or scared?' he asked when told the news. Joe Douglas, Lewis and Burrell's manager, was cut dead in the hotel foyer by Christie. 'What's wrong? we've always been friends,' Douglas asked Christie.

The rolling grey skies over Zurich had forecast a spectacular cloudburst all day, and sure enough just as the meeting was getting underway the rain began falling in sheets, thunder rattled around the surrounding mountains and high winds whipped water up into everybody's faces. The conditions, including a wind of 1.4 miles per second into the sprinters faces, nullified the advantage of the new track at the Letzigrund Stadium,

which had been laid at the cost of £330,000 and was designed to turn a very fast surface into a world record one. Now everyone was just racing for pride.

The first shock came in the heats. Christie cruised comfortably through the opening one but in the second and third races Burrell and Mitchell struggled to make it. Indeed, Burrell only scraped in the final after the toss of the coin while Mitchell had to rely on being a fastest loser. But there was still a big-name casualty. Andre Cason, second in the 1993 World Championships to Christie, was the unlucky one who called wrong

'Often I don't recognize the man called Linford Christie who I read about in the papers'

in the spin-off with Burrell.

As the sprinters settled into their blocks for the final, there was a crackle of anticipation around the Stadium which had been fully sold out and, despite the conditions, was full to overflowing. The gun fired and the fastest men in the world rose out of their blocks. Christie was out slower than Mitchell, to his right in lane five, and Jon Drummond, another American to his left in lane three. But after 40 metres Christie unleashed those long, high-stepping strides of his and cruised past Mitchell and Drummond for a magnificent victory in 10.05 seconds. Drummond finished second in 10.15, Adeniken third in 10.22, Mitchell fourth in 10.23 and Burrell a sad seventh in 10.39.

'Am I the best in the world?' Christie pondered in the post-race press conference. 'Go back and ask Carl Lewis what he thinks now. I'm old but I'm not cold. I am the undisputed Number 1. There was a lot of pressure on me because as the World, Olympic and European champion everybody wants to beat me. I proved tonight I am a great champion. There were great guys out there. I'm really happy. I loved this one.'

(following pages) Sprinting in the rain: on his way to beating Dennis Mitchell (no. 240) and Jon Drummond in Zurich, 1994

The chairman:
Linford finds
time to sit
down for a
moment during
a whirlwind
1994

Christie's performance earned him praise from some unexpected quarters. 'In the conditions that was the greatest 100 metre dash I've ever seen,' said Tony Campbell, Mitchell's agent, shaking his head in admiration. One Finnish statistician worked out that Christie's performance was worth 9.93 seconds without the wind. Without the rain and in warm conditions? Who knows. Would Christie have broken Burrell's record? 'I don't worry about world records,' he said. 'They come and go. It's titles I want, and victories. I set out my plans this year and my record speaks for itself.

'It may have been raining on the other guys, but the sun was shining on me. It gave me as much pleasure to win as any other race I can remember. I wish Carl Lewis could have been here as well. He has accused me of ducking him. But then he pulls out of Zurich saying he had a stomach upset after drinking tap water in St Petersburg. He's got enough experience not to do that. He was the one ducking me. Perhaps now

the sort of thing I get. I don't need it, no-one does. I seriously thought about calling it a day after the European Championships.

'I do care about British athletics and, if we do not want it to go the same way as British tennis, some serious planning has got to be done now. I am only going to be around another couple of years and when I go, there is going to be a big hole left.'

No-one will argue with that point. Christie enjoys a popularity unprecedented in British sport. Kids love him – he regularly comes out top in ratings lists – and adults refer to him as a point of excellence. In the *Mail on Sunday* he came second only to Terry Waite in a poll designed to find 'Great British Achievement'.

A Christie appearance at any meeting in Britain results in screams. The high screech of young female fans, who finally have a chance to see this hero in person. And not so young female fans. 'Show me where Linford is,' one blue-rinsed middle-aged lady from the Shires said to a commissioner at Crystal Palace last July as she was shown to her seat in the stand. 'The only reason I've come tonight is to see his lunch box. He makes me go all funny everytime I see him.'

Linford Christie undoubtedly has presence. The ramrod posture that makes him seem much taller than his 6 feet 2 inches, the big smile that he displays to the crowd on his laps of honour, the reactions to victory, sometimes outrageous, sometimes subdued. This is the Linford Christie the public want to believe in, not the embittered individual who the press have to deal with.

'I am only going to be around another couple of years and when I go, there is going to be a big hole left'

the Americans will realize who is Number 1.'

Yet even now, in this moment of great triumph, Christie remained a tortured soul, the Mr Angry of World Athletics as all his old paranoia bubbled to the surface. His annoyance with the Americans had subsided and instead he turned on Peter Radford. Christie was still seething at the comments he had made during the European Championships. 'I didn't like what he said about me. I didn't break any rules so why should he have a go at me? I've spent eight or nine years giving everything to athletics and trying to put the Great back into Britain. I've won all the major titles. I've always tried to be positive. And this is

Christie flew over to Canada for the Commonwealth Games via Brussels where another impressive victory in 10.03 seconds indicated that he was in shape to break evens for the first time this summer. What Christie found in Victoria was a town that likes to call itself 'more like England than England'. Not that Christie was able to enjoy it. He flew 15 hours across nine time zones to be lauded as 'the marquee athlete of the Games' by organizers but barely had time to shake hands with the local dignitaries, race, collect his medal and fly back to Europe to resume the serious business of making money.

In the event, Christie the Athlete was magnificent. After an adequate start, he accelerated to a dazzling 9.91 seconds, while the rest of the field held on for whatever might be left in his wake. The silver went to Horace Dove-Edwin of Sierra Leone in 10.02 (although he was later disqualified for taking anabolic steroids), the bronze to Michael Green of Jamaica. Adeniken, the sprinter involved in the Zurich brawl, was a shadow of his usual self, though it is unlikely even fully fit he would have challenged Christie.

Even Christie's fellow competitors were in awe, breaking a sprinter's rule which requires them to maintain confidence in their ability to beat anyone in the world on any given day. 'Linford couldn't be beaten today,' said Green. 'In fact at the moment I think he's probably unbeatable.'

At the press conference afterwards, there were of course the inevitable questions about his age and motivation. 'This hasn't become a "Another Day at The Office" sport for me,' he replied. 'I still enjoy competing and putting my neck on the line. It's a lot harder to get the adrenaline going, but it's still there, the heart reacts and I still keep winning.

'The age thing? Age is in the mind. What do they say – you are as young as the woman you feel.'

Even Linford Christie, however, is not Superman. When he returned to Europe he appeared to have left his best form somewhere over the Atlantic. At the IAAF Grand Prix final in Paris, he looked tired, and was unable to call upon that mid-race burst which had swept him to so many famous victories. Dennis Mitchell sensing that, nipped Christie on the line, winning by one-hundredth of a second in 10.12. But a disbelieving Christie demanded to study a photograph of the finish before he accepted the verdict.

But this 1994 season, the mother of all seasons because it was so crowded, was a marathon, not a sprint and two weeks later Christie knew he must have recovered his form for when he led Britain in the World Cup final at Crystal Palace. Like the great competitor he is, he did not let his country down, winning the 100 metres and anchoring the 4x100 metres to victory as Britain

finished third, a remarkable performance as their preparations had been overshadowed by the

fall-out from the Diane Modahl drugs affair which had consumed the sport since the Commonwealth Games.

When the press conference for the 100 metres was finished, Christie attempted to leave the hall. He could not. He was mobbed by kids

(following pages)
Straining for the tape: Dennis Mitchell nips Christie on the line at the IAAF Grand Prix Final, Paris, 1994

John Regis hands the baton over to Linford and starts celebrating Britain's victory in the 4×100 metres relay at the World Cup, Crystal Palace, 1994

and adults, white and black, people who knew him and those who said they did. He gave autographs, smiled, nodded, shook hands, signed more autographs, posed for pictures with anyone who eluded the security force and sidled up to him. In the end, a police escort was called for so he could escape. Athletes inadvertently caught up in the mêlée were overwhelmed, sharing in the awe-struck crush that envelops Christie wherever he goes these days. Nuff Respect.

Linford Christie
Major international honours

1986

1st   European Indoor Championships 200m
1st   Commonwealth Games 100m
1st   European Championships 200m

1987

1st   European Cup 100m
1st   European Cup 200m
3rd   World Championships 100m

1988

1st   European Indoor Championships 60m
3rd   European Indoor Championships 200m
2nd   Olympic Games 100m
2nd   Olympic Games 4x100m relay

1989

1st   European Cup 100m
1st   World Cup 100m

1990

1st   European Indoor Championships 60m
1st   Commonwealth Games 100m
1st   European Championships 100m
3rd   European Championships 200m

1991

2nd   World Indoor Championships 60m
2nd   World Indoor Championships 200m
1st   European Cup 100m
3rd   World Championships 4x100m relay

1992

1st   Olympic Games 100m
1st   World Cup 100m
2nd   World Cup 200m

1993

1st   European Cup 100m
1st   World Championships 100m
2nd   World Championships 4x100m relay

1994

1st   European Championships 100m
1st   Commonwealth Games 100m
1st   European Cup 100m
1st   World Cup 100m